JOHN TORODE'S
BEEF

JOHN TORODE'S
'BEEF'

and other bovine matters

photographs by Jason Lowe

Quadrille

To Jess and the kids

When I opened Smiths of Smithfield in 2000, I was already well into my love affair with all things beef, but eight years on the relationship is now well and truly cemented. It is the one subject I can discuss till the cows come home (ho ho) but it is also an area that many people feel very confused about – both in what to buy, and then how to get the best out of the meat they have bought. After many years of thinking about it and discussing it, here it is: the cookbook I felt compelled to write. It's aimed at everyone – home cooks as well as the odd chef.

JOHN TORODE'S BEEF has been written because I believe that good food should be accessible to all people. That is the simple reason. I hope it will give you the confidence not just to cook beef but also to buy beef and recognise what is good and, more importantly, what ain't.

When given the chance to write this book, I really wanted to pour out all I know and love about beef. I have tried to be as helpful as possible without being a food bore or getting too technical; I don't want the book to be scary, so I have given just as much advice as is practical. At the least you will find a huge range of recipes, cooking tips and advice on how to buy good beef, and that is the best start.

The bottom line is bloody good food, food that people want to eat. Some recipes are 15-minute wonders and some are quite testing – it wouldn't be a good book if they weren't!

Most, though, are mine, learnt from simple home cooking, because rightly or wrongly I feel restaurant recipes belong in a restaurant. Restaurant chefs cook differently, their kitchens are run differently; their recipes are practised and concise and leave little room for mucking around. I am not precious – if you want to add something or take something away, go for it. Change the recipes, have fun, and if anything works better than my recipe, send me a note. I shall burn it! (Just joking – I would appreciate it, we all need to learn new tricks.)

Food, cooking, kitchens, mates, dinner tables – they are good things but good things are not always constant. Good food moves and changes depending on your mood, your friends – even the weather can affect it a little. If we are honest, we all have our 'best' recipes. Whether it is a great salad, a big barbied burger or a beautiful posh pastry dish like beef Wellington, the recipe has generally taken a lot of practice to reach what we feel is perfection. What I'm saying is: if a recipe in this book doesn't turn out so well for you one day, don't dismiss it, give it another go.

Finally, a few general points on the recipes. All pepper used is freshly milled black pepper unless the recipe states otherwise; eggs are medium size while the tablespoons are 15ml and teaspoons 5ml. The cow symbols ☛ indicate how many people each dish serves. An outlined symbol indicates a half portion.

'SOME BASICS'

Beef is for eating and comes from beef cattle; milk comes from dairy cows.

Dairy cows are primarily those black and white ones that look like they are having fun, whereas beef cattle are most of the beautiful big butch ones that stand and stare at you.

THE BULL: the bloke. He is there to breed, that's his job. Older ones pull carts and are not eaten, they are as tough as old boots.

THE STEER: a bull with his bits chopped off, used for beef production. He can't do much but eat and sleep, poor bugger.

THE HEIFER: a female. They give birth each year but a heifer is primarily for beef production. She gets to play with the bull.

THE COW: a female used for dairy – that is, milking. They are usually Friesians and Holsteins and have udders. The meat from them is not that good, hence the expression 'old cow'.

THE VEALER: usually the males from a dairy herd. Dairy cattle, as I have said above, don't grow into great beef but if slaughtered young make great veal.

So much of what I have read about beef is pointed toward the selected and lucky few, who have bags of cash and can afford to spend huge swathes of money at farmers' markets, online and on other alternative forms of shopping. Good meat is not cheap, but it should not break the bank either, and there are plenty of butchers who are more than willing to give you sound advice to add to mine as to what you should buy for each dish. There are a few simple rules:

🐂 All meat is muscle, each muscle works at a different rate and holds a different weight.

🐂 The muscles that do all the work, such as shin, leg and clod (shoulder), need long, slow cooking to break down the tissue and should always be served well done.

🐂 The muscles that do less work (rump, fore rib) will be more tender and can be grilled and fried, but slowly, not quickly. When cooked that bit longer to medium they will be more tender.

🐂 The muscles that do no work, the sirloin and fillet, can be cooked quickly and served very rare as they do not have the structure of a working muscle.

Great beef, regardless of where on the beast it is from, should have fine rivers of fat running through the muscle so that, as it cooks, the fat melts and keeps the meat moist.

A good beef animal will be about 35-40 months old and a real biggy. It should have had a nice life, grazing calmly and free of stress. It should have a well-formed body but, unlike an athlete, would have had time to lay fat in the muscle. An animal that's been worked will be tough, regardless of how long you cook it.

The last part of its life is important too. A great animal will be ruined if its slaughter is stressful. The kill, as it is known, should be calm and quick, and no other beast should know what is happening before or afterwards. A stressed kill pumps adrenalin into the blood, reducing the flesh to grainy, chewy, watery lumps of bitter meat. To prevent this, good butchers buy from small slaughterhouses rather than big units.

Value

The value of each cut is determined by customer demand. In Asia offal is extremely expensive because people prize it, whereas in the West fillet is highly prized because it is so tender. (In reality there are far better cuts than fillet, you just have to know how to cook them.) It is all about supply and demand – there are only two fillets of, say, 4kg in a 300kg beast, so it is a rarity, whereas a hunk of shin weighing 30kg is not sought after (well, not until now that is).

Flavour

The most worked (and well-lived) muscles will deliver the best flavour, until you start to take ageing into account. However the rule of thumb is that the brisket, for example, will taste a lot richer than the rib or fillet.

Ageing

This is the technique used to mature beef and make steaks tender. I only like beef aged in the open air; the Australians do it differently, as do a lot of American producers. In open air ageing the meat remains attached to the bone and hangs, usually in pieces, including the fore rib, sirloin, rump and fillet. Each piece benefits in richness, flavour and tenderness from a different period of ageing – the fillet about 18 days, the sirloin and the rib 24-28 days, and the rump 30-plus. That is, to me, the rule. Should you want a steak, try to buy it from someone who hangs their meat.

Warning!!! About the word 'matured'. Many supermarkets put the phrase 'matured for 14 (or even 21) days' on their pre-packed meat. I am yet to understand how this works as their meat is all boned 24 hours after slaughter and then packed in plastic bags to 'mature'. The plastic bags are kept in large plastic crates in huge cool rooms. The meat still contains a lot of blood, which is then absorbed by the fat. I find that these steaks just retain water, which comes out during cooking, leaving you with dry meat.

'BUYING BEEF'

Please try to find a local butcher you can get to know and trust. This really helps when buying any type of meat. As you build a relationship with them, they will point you towards the best cuts and specials in any given season.

Having said that, I am also a realist. I know full well that people do go to the supermarket, and the majority of Britons do most of their weekly shop in huge stores. With this in mind, throughout the book I'm giving you lots of hints and tips. They are not there to scare the pants off you, but to inform and educate. This is a cookbook after all, not a lecture. So I'm happy to tell you that one thing the supermarkets do really well is cuts for stewing and braising. You can't go wrong with great hunks of shin – I make the best rendang in the world using shin; it can't be beaten for flavour and texture.

I reckon the current trend for organic food is The Greatest Marketing Campaign on Earth. Food that is labelled 'organic' is often expensive, often inaccessible, and not always as it may seem. While farming in a way that supports the environment is a good idea, flying 'organic' produce halfway around the world, then packing it and carting it all around the country rather defeats the object.

However, I do believe it is important to know where your beast comes from, what it has been fed and how it has lived. So, in all the time I have been seriously buying beef, I have supported the Rare Breeds Survival Trust, a conservation charity devoted to Britain's native livestock breeds. It is a group of great farmers, breeders and producers – I like my farmers and I like the people I buy from.

Let's make no bones about it, this meat is expensive, but quality delivers yield. Beef that has reached its full lifecycle and is treated well and then hung will not be tough, watery or stringy – that only happens when beef cattle are too young and go off to the block stressed and badly handled.

My advice is to find a good high street butcher to buy your beef from: there are some suggestions on page 250. They are great people, they love what they do (they must with the hassle they have suffered over the past decade or so), so please support them.

'THE BREEDS'

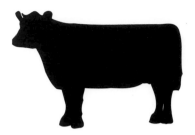

Aberdeen Angus

The true Angus has a smooth, solid black coat. The bull is huge and majestic and has been the pride of Scotland, but unfortunately few pure breeds now exist. They are slow growers, and the promotion of Angus as great for eating has lead to commercial cross-breeding. It's a shame. The few times I have eaten true Angus it has been a good hunk of beef.

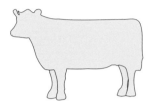

Charolais

The commercial breed that dominates the American and Australian landscape, these animals like the heat. Unlike many of the traditional British breeds, they are also good at being herded and produce consistent quality beef, but for me they are not the best.

Belgian Blue

This is the body builder of beef, and favoured in America. It is a massive animal, has an all-white coat with a blue tinge and a stance like a bulldog. In the United Kingdom, Belgian Blues are bred with dairy cattle to get beef from the boys.

Dexter

Fast becoming the hobby farm choice, Dexters are small bodied (tiny, really, in the land of big beasts) but they are calm and easy to look after. They are notoriously bad for milk but give truly delicious beef. A well-grown, well-slaughtered, well-hung piece of Dexter beef will be sweet and smoky – one of my very favourites. Oh, and if you want to look out for one, they are black, sometimes with a tiny flash of white on the face.

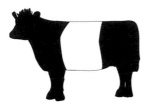

Galloway

Small-to-medium-sized beef cattle with a black body. The best – the Belted Galloways – have a big white belt wrapped around their middle. They can survive in harsh environments and have done well on poorer soil in places like the New Forest and Exmoor. The beef is sweet and has a good chew, great for rump steak. When matured over 30 days, the meat goes soft in texture and flavour, rather like great cheese.

Highland

Yep, you got it, from the Scottish Highlands. And because it is cold and wet there, they have large feet, thick flanks, and a big, brownish-red, woolly coat. Some have beautiful long horns, too. Slaughtered young, they are better to look at than eat, but let them grow to as old as four years, wandering free and doing their own thing, and they will be good hefty meat producers, with large joints of smoky, well-marbled beef.

Hereford

It's not difficult to work out where these come from: yep, Herefordshire. They are big, beautiful animals with brown coats and large white faces. Many look like they are wearing long white socks, though they do have short, stumpy legs. Some even have little horns. I love this meat when it is well-produced, but rarely do you see Hereford beef sold as a pure breed; it gets mixed with commercial breeds and put on supermarket shelves.

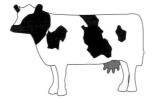

Holstein

The classic black and white cow – the ones that graze away as we drive past but you suspect they all stand up and have a conversation once we have gone. Holstein females produce milk. The males are great for veal but not much chop for mature beef, as their middles are not that long and they have big bums.

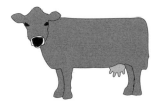

Jersey

The Jersey is white, almost cream in colour, and not at all good beef cattle. It makes good cream and lots of milk but the breed really leaves very little for the blokes to do!

Lincoln Red

Native to the Wolds, these were the girls that made the milk for the great stilton cheese of old but I believe this is no longer the case. They are meat-producing beasts now, and have proved to be one of Britain's greatest exports as they are resistant to tsetse fly, making them a hit in Canada, America and the West Indies. They have reddish brown coats but no horns.

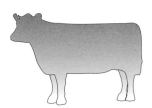

Limousin

Probably the most successful breed of commercial beef, now often crossed with the Angus and the Shorthorn.

Longhorn

Prominent in the Midlands, these mighty beasts have long horns and thick necks to carry that great weight. They are a mix of dark and light brown, mottled and beautiful. Another great export to the US, they love grass but when slaughtered too early the meat is nowhere near what it should be. Left to grow and graze on grass – wow! What a piece of beef!

North Devon

Devonshires, or Red Rubies as they are sometimes known, come from down Bristol way and have a red-brown, almost down-like coat. Not a big animal in the world of beef, they are shaggy and scary looking, but calm. They produce great, well-marbled meat when left to fend for themselves.

Welsh Black

These are big black animals, but they do have a wash of white on the end of their tails, and sometimes on their faces. The Welsh Black Society protects the breed and produces books each year detailing who has what. The beef is good; they are also good dairy cows. Thick black curly coats allow them to survive the harsh weather of the Welsh hills and valleys.

Shorthorn

A legend among the beef-producing animals, the Shorthorn has a coat that ranges from white to brown but is broken up with rust coloured markings. Its horns are small, as the name suggests, and like the Longhorn, it needs a good three years to make great beef. It's not bad as dairy cattle either.

White Park

Majestic yet lovable, not only is the great White Park one of the best breeds for beef, it is also the symbol of the Rare Breeds Survival Trust. These animals are massive; they produce huge long loins, big ribs, and some of the best steaks I have ever eaten.

'BEEF CUTS'

Beef fillet
The fillet of any animal that walks on all fours will be the tenderest, most prized piece of meat for the mere fact that it is the only muscle that a quadruped does not use. Of the 145kg of meat and bone on each side of a beast (whether it be steer or heifer) only some 2.7kg is fillet.

Fillet comes from inside the ribcage and at its thinnest point is attached to the kidneys; feel where your kidneys are and then think about a muscle that runs up along the middle of your spine – that is the fillet. It is surrounded by a film of fat, most of which can be prized away with the fingers. The silver skin that sits at the head end of the fillet should then be eased away little by little with a very sharp knife.

The fillet has three main sections. The flat end, called the tail, is classically used for stroganoff (yes, proper quality stroganoff) and steak tartare, which is chopped, seasoned and served raw with toast – so delicious. The head, which is the thick end, is used for chateaubriand or beef Wellington, or simply as a roast (though it will need a little fat left in the creases should you wish to do that). Once the tail and head are removed we are left with the centre. This central fillet is for steaks – the great fillet steak, tournedos (as in Rossini with truffle and foie gras) and for carpaccio.

Sirloin & rump
The great steaks, including T-bone, come from the sirloin and the rump – the huge hunk of meat that forms the back of the animal. Many beefers like myself prefer steaks with the flavour of a rump or a sirloin, rather than fillet. If you buy one as a big hunk and want to cut it into steaks, push the hunk together and place it fat-side down before you slice it: you will get a better, more even cut.

Flank/skirt
A bloody great big hunk of meat that is often relegated to the stewpot and mince, even though its sits beautifully underneath the sirloin. The French do not relegate this tasty cut, however – they trim it and bash it to make bavette steak. Although it is a little chewy, if trimmed and marinated it can be used for a barbecue.

In real terms, flank/skirt is the belly of the beast. For fun, buy a hunk of flank, roast it slowly for three hours and serve it with some green herb sauce – yum. The further down the belly you go, the leaner the meat gets, so it can be a bit tough. It is good for stews and casseroles that have lots of gravy. Should you not be able to buy brisket for salt beef, this is the baby; the Americans prefer flank/skirt to make pastrami as its even thickness means it smokes well.

Neck & clod
A good-sized beast has to eat a lot (about 8kg of feed for each kg of animal) so the neck and clod muscles endure a lot of activity, making them really tasty. That is why good mince makes great ragu and sauces and the brilliant burger is so stunning. There is little you can do besides mince or slow-cook the neck and clod, and many a big store sells them as stewing steak or braising steak.

Chuck & blade

This has to be the most-used muscle in the whole beast, and as such it gives great lean, fibrous meat in huge pieces. Blade, if sliced very thinly and marinated, is good on the barbecue. It also works well for things like satay, as long as it is cut into thin, thin strips. I love blade left on the bone and braised and then stripped off and shredded – it has great flavour. This mighty hunk of meat also makes fantastic pies.

Brisket

Few people understand the importance of brisket. It sits at the bottom of the neck and runs along the ribs. Until it drops (think of very fat men and their double chins), the beast really should not be slaughtered as the meat will not have the structure of great beef.

Brisket is not a tender piece of meat at all but the flavour – wow! It is used for making the most prized type of salt beef, which makes the very best salt beef sandwich (after rib five it is no longer kosher, and good salt beef is always kosher).

On a young beast the brisket will be flavourless and fatty, however an older animal that has had plenty of time in the field, moved around and fed and chewed and worked, will give brisket that is a truly delicious delight.

Shin & leg

Those who know me well get why I love this cut of beef. On or off the bone, it has to be the ultimate in braising and stewing meat. It is what it says on the tin: the top of the bottom of the leg and the shin (in human terms the calf and forearm). These muscles are wrapped around huge bones, which are filled with delicious marrow bone. The thing I really love, however, is the meat's structure. As it cooks, the collagen that holds the muscle together and keeps it attached to the bone melts away, leaving moist meat and a delicious sticky sauce. On a vealer this cut is the osso bucco, or bone and hole.

Luscious oxtail

The Brits were in great danger of losing the beloved oxtail when beef on the bone was banned. For over a year I had the odd one smuggled to my home to make stews and pudding. In complete contrast to the fillet, the oxtail is a gelatinous and tough piece of meat that sits sparingly on the bones that make up the tail. Once in my life I have boned a tail, then stuffed it and rolled it, and it was delicious. But for me this is an on-the-bone, 'stew me for a few hours and then I am ready' type of meat. It makes the best of sticky, thick gravies, thanks to the joints along the tail and the amount of gelatine the meat produces. It also makes complex, sweet sauces that are fabulous served with fish like brill and turbot. Most oxtail is now sold jointed and ready to cook, however it can be bought whole and is easy enough to joint yourself with a good hefty knife, as long as you strike in the joints of the bones.

Note Australian readers should refer to the poster on the inside of this book's jacket for corresponding cuts of beef and their local names.

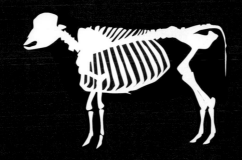

STOCKS SOUPS & GRAVY

Proper stock is a great thing. As an apprentice I was taught to make a true beef and veal stock which, I admit, needs time, patience and a big pot. The great thing about making any stock is that once you've got all the flavour into the liquid, you can strain it then put it back on the stove and boil it and boil it until it's a syrup. Culinarily this is called glace de viande, or glaze of meat – effectively it's a stock cube. I freeze them like ice cubes and bring them out when making a sauce. I find the whole process satisfying but understand why some may think it's a drag. If you want to make a soup or sauce in a hurry and need to cheat, there are tubs of stock and concentrate in all sorts of sachets, tubes and cubes, but ensure you buy a good one with no E numbers lurking in it.

'BEEF STOCK'

Makes 5 litres
10kg beef bones
4 large carrots, roughly chopped
4 large onions, roughly chopped
vegetable oil
2 heads garlic, halved
1 bunch celery, roughly chopped
2 large leeks, roughly chopped
a few bay leaves

Shin bones are ideal for this as their natural gelatine makes the stock especially sticky. Instead of 10kg beef bones, you could use a half-and-half mixture of beef and veal bones and add a pig's foot.

Heat the oven to 200°C (gas 6). Put the bones in a large bowl or sink and cover with cold water. Add a handful of salt and leave for 10 minutes – this will draw out the blood.

Throw the water away and put the bones in a large roasting pan with the carrots and onions. Sprinkle with a little oil and roast for about 40 minutes or until brown (and I mean brown).

Tip everything from the roasting pan into a stockpot. Add the remaining ingredients, cover with water, and bring the stock to a rolling boil. Pour in about 500ml cold water, which sets any fat as it rises to the surface. Adjust the heat so that the stock just ticks over and start skimming the grey foam that will come to the surface. (As an apprentice we used to put our egg shells in the stock as they would help collect all the muck.)

Keep the stock ticking over for 8 hours, skimming as necessary. Strain the stock and leave it to cool overnight, so any remaining fat settles on top and is easy to lift off and throw away, leaving you with a good clear, well-flavoured stock.

veal bones
beef bones
water
1 large Gastro Mirepoix of fresh
veg (carrots, onions, leeks,
celery)
herb stalks (basil and parsley,
can be found in pastry fridge)
5 heads garlic, cut in half

This is the veal stock recipe from Quaglino's and Mezzo. We would use 200kg of bones each night and the boilers would hold 150 litres and the Bratt pan (a large catering pot that tilts to allow pouring) 100 litres! Stocks would tick over as we slept, then early in the morning they were strained and we would have access to good clear stock right away – no OXO cubes in my kitchens! Looking back, I love the regimental nature of this recipe, so I have included it as it stood in the kitchen. There's no need to make 150 litres, but this tasty stock is great for general home cooking too. You'll need about 3kg bones and one head of garlic to make 3 litres of stock.

Lightly brown bones in oven. Do not burn.

Place bones in boiler or Bratt pan.

Add water and bring to the boil, skimming frequently.

Simmer for 15 minutes, skimming frequently and then add mirepoix, herbs and garlic.

These stocks should be on 1.00pm. These can be simmered until 11.30pm. They should then be left on low heat until 8.00am next morning. The stocks should then be passed off and put in tall pans to reduce.

Inform kitchen porters that the boiler and Bratt pan are ready for cleaning.

NB1: Do not boil stocks as they will go cloudy and greasy.
NB2: The bratt pan must be cleaned by 7.45am to enable crustacea to cook their shellfish. Under no circumstances should the sauce section prevent crustacea from using the bratt pan. It is used first and foremost for cooking off shellfish.

'FRENCH ONION SOUP WITH GRUYÈRE CROUTE'

100g butter
4 large onions, thinly sliced
salt and pepper
20ml malt vinegar
20ml brandy (optional)
600ml beef stock (page 22)
4 slices baguette
150g gruyère cheese, grated

This is a meal rather than just a big bowl of soup. Onion soup is one of those great things that needs to be dripping off your chin, so don't try to be dainty with this soup – slurp and munch instead. Be careful with the bowls and the bread when they first come out of the oven – they will be super-hot. Cheat, if you wish, by grilling the bread and dropping it into the soup.

Heat the oven to 200°C (gas 6). Melt the butter in a saucepan, add the onions, a good grind of pepper and some salt, and cook slowly until golden – about 5 minutes. Add the vinegar, stir well and you will see the onions really getting brown – keep the heat high and keep stirring, it will smell great.

When the onions are sticky and brown, pour in the brandy, if using. Strike a match and flame the pan, then pour in the stock immediately so you don't burn off all the booze – I like to taste it on the back of the throat. Bring to the boil and reduce the heat so the soup simmers slowly for a good 20 minutes.

Meanwhile, put the sliced bread into the oven for a few minutes to crisp up.

Pour the soup into individual ovenproof bowls and float the bread on top so that it nearly covers the surface of the soup. Sprinkle the cheese over the bread, then carefully transfer the bowls to the oven for 10 minutes or until the cheese bubbles and turns golden brown.

Now the bowls are HOT, so watch it when serving.

'CONSOMMÉ, POACHED EGG AND TRUFFLE OIL'

1 carrot
1 celery stick
1 shallot
salt and pepper
300g lean minced beef
2 egg whites
4 ice cubes, crushed
800ml good quality beef stock
    (page 22)

to serve

4 eggs
splash of vinegar
2 tsp truffle oil
1-2 tbsp finely chopped chives

This recipe needs great stock. It is one dish where you really should try and make your own.

Put the carrot, celery, shallot and some salt and pepper in a food processor and blend until the veg are finely chopped. Add the minced beef, egg whites and ice, and blend again.

Combine the stock and meat mixture in a large saucepan over a low heat. You want to slowly heat the stock so that the meat floats to the top, creating a raft (a bit of professional speak there!). This will flavour the stock and make it beautifully clear.

Next increase the heat a little so that the liquid barely simmers for 30 minutes – you do not want it to boil at all. Then turn off the heat and leave it to sit while you poach the eggs. NEVER STIR OR THAT WILL BE THAT AND YOU WILL BE EATING DRY MINCE SOUP – NOT GOOD.

Poach the eggs in a large saucepan with a little vinegar added to the water. Meanwhile, heat your serving bowls.

Strain the consommé gently – preferably through a muslin cloth, but most important is that you do it slowly. Put a poached egg in the bottom of each bowl and pour the soup over. Sprinkle with the truffle oil and chopped chives and serve.

If preferred you can make the consommé in advance and store it in glass in the refrigerator for up to 5 days, or in the freezer for up to 6 months.

'TRUFFLE SOUP WITH PASTRY TOPS'

900ml consommé (page 27)

1 large truffle, well brushed

1 egg, beaten

about 200g ready-rolled puff
    pastry

This is a classic restaurant dish that looks fantastic when served in a lion-head bowl. The soup has to be warm or the puff pastry will melt into the bowls rather than rising in a majestic way. Make the consommé a day before serving.

Heat the oven to 200°C (gas 6). Warm the consommé in a saucepan. Take your serving bowls and shave some truffle into each. Cover with the consommé.

Brush the egg around the rim of each bowl. Cut the pastry into circles slightly bigger than the top of the bowl. Lay the pastry over the bowls and press to seal.

Put the bowls on a baking tray and place in the oven for about 20 minutes. The pastry should puff up like a balloon as the soup heats. When done, the pastry should be crisp on top and the underside soggy from the steam of the soup.

Take the hot bowls carefully to the table. When your guests open the pastry lids, the room will fill with the heady scent of truffle.

'MUSHROOM SOUP WITH MUSHROOM TOAST'

800g mixture chestnut and flat field mushrooms, cut in chunks if large
90g butter
1 small onion, roughly chopped
1 celery stick, roughly chopped
2 leeks, roughly chopped
salt and pepper
20g dried ceps (porcini), crushed to a powder
2 garlic cloves, crushed
100g potato, peeled
3 thyme sprigs
1 bay leaf
2 litres beef stock (page 22)
200ml double cream

mushroom toasts
drizzle of olive oil
1 banana shallot, diced
1 handful chopped flat-leaf parsley
6 slices sourdough or similar artisan-made bread
1 handful grated gruyère or cheddar cheese

I really bloody hate thin, tasteless soups that are for diet purposes only and not for taste. This soup has few calories, but has true beefy mushroom flavour from the dried mushrooms and beef stock. If you are going to use bought beef stock, buy double and, before you start to make the soup, bring it to the boil and reduce it by half to get a better, more concentrated flavour.

Set aside about 150g fresh mushrooms for topping the toasts.

Melt 40g butter in a large saucepan and cook the onion, celery and leek until soft but not coloured. Add some salt and pepper, then the crushed ceps and garlic, and cook for a minute or so. Add the larger batch of fresh mushrooms, and cook, stirring, for a few minutes, until they are soft and smell like grilled mushrooms. Add the potatoes, thyme and bay, and stir until they are fragrant.

Pour over the stock, bring the pan to the boil and cook for 15 minutes. Turn off the heat, discard the herbs, then purée the soup to the consistency you like, using a blender or food processor.

To make the toasts, heat the grill. Take the remaining mushrooms, season them well, drizzle with a little olive oil and place them under the grill. Cook for 4-5 minutes on each side. Meanwhile, heat another 50g butter in a pan and sweat the shallot over a medium heat. Chop the grilled mushrooms roughly and add to the shallot. Cook for 2 minutes, then add the chopped parsley and give the mixture a good season with some salt and pepper.

Toast the bread on one side only under the grill. Turn the bread over and spoon the fried mushroom mixture on to the uncooked side so that all the juice is soaked up by the bread. Cover with the grated cheese and grill until bubbling.

Bring the soup back to the boil and add the cream. Taste and adjust the seasoning if needed, then serve with the toasts.

'RICH BEEF & BARLEY BROTH'

1kg beef shin
1 large onion
1 large carrot
1 turnip
400ml beef stock (page 22)
1 heaped tsp sea salt
ground white pepper
1 tbsp pearl barley
1 large handful chopped parsley

Cut the meat into pieces 3cm square and drop them into a bowl of cool water for half an hour. This soaking process removes any excess blood that would make the soup bitter and cloudy, however if you are using kosher beef you can skip this stage.

Meanwhile, peel the vegetables and cut them into pieces about the same size as the meat.

Put a heavy-based casserole over a medium heat and add the stock and vegetables. Drain the meat and add it to the pan with the salt and some white pepper. Bring to a simmer and add the pearl barley. Reduce the heat a little so the liquid just simmers (the meat will go tough if you let it boil) and cook for $1\frac{1}{2}$ hours. While the soup cooks, use a ladle to skim off any impurities that float to the surface. Alternatively, you can put the pot of soup in a 180°C (gas 4) oven and leave it to cook for 2 hours while you go and have a walk or something – personally I think that's a nicer way of doing it.

Stir the parsley into the soup (the result is rather like a stew, not very brothy) just before serving it with lots of hot bread.

'ONION GRAVY'

Makes 500ml

20ml dripping or vegetable oil

2kg large white onions

salt and pepper

1 tbsp malt vinegar

50g butter

50g plain flour

300ml beef stock (page 22)

When I do a roast at home, I try and keep the fat drained from the joint as I like to use it for cooking later, just like my nanna with her dripping tin. This, for me, will deliver the very best flavour in this recipe, but that's just me being a dreamer – you can always use vegetable oil if preferred. This recipe will serve at least six people (I like lots of gravy) and leftovers are easily used – served with faggots (page 231) or sausages, or stirred into sauce poivrade (page 217). You'll find my nanna's gravy recipe on page 153.

Place a good sized saucepan over a high heat and add the dripping or oil. Slice the onions and add them to the pan. Season with salt and pepper and stir until wilted.

Add the vinegar and continue to cook, stirring often, for at least 10 minutes, until the onions have some colour. Add the butter and stir until it has melted. Sprinkle in the flour and keep cooking and stirring for 5 minutes.

Pour in the stock and give a good stir, scraping the bottom of the pot to take off all the crust that has built up from the flour (this is full of flavour and will thicken the gravy). Bring to the boil and cook for 6-7 minutes, stirring continuously. Taste and adjust the seasoning as necessary before serving.

CARPACCIO

The great carpaccio is famously named after the painter Vittore Carpaccio, who loved to contrast red and white. Well that's the story, anyway. Many will argue that carpaccio should be simply raw beef fillet sliced very thinly and served with a sprinkle of olive oil and lemon juice, pepper and salt. Delicious as that may be, come on! We can be a little more exciting than that. Here you'll find some fantastic toppings for carpaccio, each of which creates a very special dish. The beef fillet you use for carpaccio should be fresh, fresh, fresh and not hung for a long period. Unlike most cuts, fillet benefits very little from time on the bone (with one exception – read on!) and it shrinks, so it costs a bloody fortune. Other things to remember: don't buy fillet in a plastic wrap or it will taste gross – and don't freeze it, or it will turn to mush.

'BASIC RECIPE: CARPACCIO'

200-260g beef fillet
good quality olive oil
salt

Take the central cut of the fillet, or the tail, which is cheaper. You need about 50-60g per person for a starter, which is not a lot. Wrap it in cling film and tighten each end like a sausage so that the beef has a shape. Put it in the fridge to cool for an hour or so before slicing and put the serving plates in the fridge too.

Just before you slice the beef, lay out the plates and put a drop or two of olive oil and a little salt on each one – it gives the beef a better depth of flavour and stops it sticking.

Trim off all the fat from the beef fillet and slice the meat as thinly as possible.

Lay four squares of cling film on the bench. Place an equal amount of sliced beef on each piece of cling film, positioning it so the slices do not overlap. Top with another sheet of cling film and press down to seal.

Using a rolling pin, gently tap the beef so that it spreads out and becomes wafer-thin – if possible about the same size as the plate you are going to serve it on.

Remove the top layer of cling film and invert the carpaccio on to a plate. Drizzle with a little olive oil and use your fingers to spread the oil all over the meat (this stops it changing colour and drying out). Now you are not in a restaurant, so a bit of artistic licence is fine, I think, but don't make it look too mucked around with, just sliced and plated.

Serve with any of the dressings or toppings you fancy on the following pages.

Classic Cream Dressing

1 medium egg
1 egg yolk
1 tbsp dijon mustard
1 tbsp shallot vinegar
1 garlic clove, crushed
200ml vegetable oil
200ml olive oil
175g parmesan cheese, grated

Whisk the whole egg, yolk, mustard, vinegar and garlic together in a large bowl until the mixture begins to thicken and turn pale. Slowly add the oils, whisking constantly, until well amalgamated. Add a little hot water if the mixture seems too thick. Stir in the grated cheese. Drizzle the dressing over the prepared plates of beef.

Cover and store the leftovers in the refrigerator for use with salads. Makes about 600ml.

Jersey Royals with Capers & Anchovies

200g Jersey Royal potatoes, scrubbed
2 tbsp olive oil
salt and pepper
1 thumbnail-sized lump butter
2 tsp capers
3 anchovy fillets preserved in oil, roughly chopped
juice of 1 lemon
a few leaves tarragon, roughly chopped

Boil the potatoes for 10 minutes, then drain. Heat the oil in a frying pan. Add the par-boiled potatoes and fry for 5-10 minutes, stirring often.

When the potatoes are coloured and tender, grind in a good amount of pepper. Add the butter and, once it has melted, add the capers and anchovies and let them sizzle for a minute or so until the capers start to pop and turn crisp.

Take the pan off the heat and pour over the lemon juice. Add the tarragon and season to taste with salt and pepper. Leave to cool slightly while you prepare your four plates of carpaccio, then serve the beef with the seasoned potatoes.

Mozzarella, Beetroot, Broad Beans & White Anchovies

2 bunches baby beetroot
100g broad beans
4 tsp red wine vinegar
150ml extra virgin olive oil
flaked sea salt and black pepper
2 large balls buffalo mozzarella
20 white anchovies, drained
hot fresh bread

Boil the beetroot in lots of water for 12-15 minutes; leave to cool in the water. In another pan, boil the beans for 2 minutes, drain and refresh in cold water.

Mix together the vinegar, 80ml olive oil and some seasoning. Scrape off the beetroot skins, cut them in half and drop in the dressing. Tear the mozzarella into pieces and scatter over the carpaccio. Follow with the beans, beetroot and anchovies. Sprinkle the cheese with a little salt. Drizzle the plates with the remaining oil. Serve with hot bread.

Watercress, Gorgonzola & Parmesan Dressing

1 egg yolk
2 tsp vinegar
2 tsp water
20g parmesan cheese, grated, plus shaved parmesan, to garnish
100ml vegetable oil
2 tbsp olive oil
4 tsp cream
salt and black pepper
100g gorgonzola cheese
50g watercress

Beat the egg yolk, vinegar, water and grated parmesan in a bowl until white. Slowly add the oils to avoid splitting, then add the cream and stir well. Taste and season with salt and pepper. Crumble the gorgonzola cheese over the carpaccio. Top with the watercress and pour a good tablespoon of dressing over each. Garnish with the shaved parmesan.

Rocket, Lemon & Truffle Oil

50g rocket
2 tsp quality olive oil
sea salt and black pepper
1 lemon, plus 4 wedges to serve
50g parmesan shavings
2 tsp truffle oil

In a bowl, dress the rocket with the olive oil, some pepper and a few flakes of sea salt and mix well. Add a little lemon juice to taste (it needs to be sharp but not enough to make you screw your eyes up). Scatter the dressed rocket over the plate of delicious fillet, then scatter with the parmesan cheese. Drizzle with the truffle oil. Grind over some more pepper and serve each plate with a wedge of lemon.

Grilled Radicchio

3 radicchio, cut in wedges
olive oil
coarse salt and cracked pepper
1 small bunch marjoram, parsley or basil
1 juicy lemon
1 handful shaved parmesan cheese

Heat the oven to 200°C (gas 6). Spread and separate the leaves of radicchio. Rub with a little olive oil and season with salt and pepper.

Heat a griddle pan until hot, and I mean hot – give it 10 minutes over a high flame so that when you add the radicchio, it sizzles. Grill the radicchio for a minute on each side, then put it in a ceramic baking dish. Drizzle with more oil, add the herbs and bake for 10 minutes.

Remove the baking dish from the oven, turn the radicchio over and, while it is hot, squeeze over the lemon. Turn and squeeze again, then leave to cool. Serve with the carpaccio and parmesan, drizzling them with all that lovely juice left in the baking dish.

Jalapeño, Mirin & Soy

The famed Nobu is a chef who has been successful in fusing South American and Japanese cuisines in his restaurants. This carpaccio is inspired by them and the most glorious yellowfin tuna dish they serve in a similar way to this. You can buy little sachets of instant dashi and make it up with water.

40ml mirin
20ml sake
30ml dark soy sauce
50ml dashi broth
2 jalapeño chillies

Mix all the liquids together and leave to one side. Slice the jalapeños and lay them out over the carpaccio like every second number on a clock. Pour the dressing over the carpaccio and leave to sit for 3 minutes before serving with chopsticks.

Black Truffles

This has to be the easiest carpaccio, but also the most decadent and costly. Few of us will ever get the chance to buy a beautiful big truffle and have the money to shave it over some raw beef, but I had to include this as it is gorgeous to look at and, when wafted past the nose, it gets me so excited. This is the only time that I recommend using well-hung beef fillet and to really spend the money on some great olive oil.

extra virgin olive oil
salt and pepper
1 large black truffle (as big as you can afford)

Rub a good quantity of oil over the top of the carpaccio and season well with salt and pepper.

Take the truffle in your right hand and a truffle slicer (look, if you can afford a truffle you can afford a truffle slicer) in your left and shave and shave, covering the plate with wafer-thin slices of truffle. Serve with a great big glass of oaky chardonnay.

'FENNEL, TOMATOES & OREGANO IN FOIL'

2 large tomatoes
2 large fennel bulbs
1 lemon, halved
1 handful fresh oregano or sage
1 tsp salt
1 tsp ground black pepper
50g butter

This makes a good barbecue accompaniment to the raw fillet. If you're not lighting the barbie you can cook the foil parcels in a 200°C (gas 6) oven.

Take two large pieces of foil approximately 30cm square and place them on a bench. Cut the tomatoes and fennel into quarters and cut the lemon in half. Take the oregano (or sage) and pick off all the leaves.

Put four pieces of tomato and four of fennel on each piece of foil and fold up the sides. Squeeze half a lemon over each then drop them inside the foil. Sprinkle with the herbs, then season with salt and pepper, adding ½ teaspoon of each to each parcel. Finally, divide the butter among the parcels and seal them.

Put the foil parcels over a nice hot barbecue and leave to cook for approximately 30 minutes. Remove from the heat and allow to cool slightly. Open the foil parcels at the table and serve with the prepared carpaccio.

'ROAST TOMATO SALAD'

1 bunch mixed herbs, such as
   sage, rosemary, thyme and
   basil stems
50g flaked sea salt
10 plum tomatoes, halved
   lengthwise
2 vine leaves
1 large preserved lemon, or
   2 baby ones
2 handfuls de-stoned olives,
   preferably large purple ones
1 handful flat-leaf parsley,
   roughly chopped
1 handful curly parsley, roughly
   chopped

dressing

3 tbsp olive oil
2 tsp walnut oil
1 tbsp balsamic vinegar
1 tsp lemon juice
½ tsp sugar
salt and pepper

English tomatoes are at their best in the last few weeks of July and the early part of August. Italian plum tomatoes, however, are around from the start of June. They are sweet and full of juice. What this recipe does is condense their juice and concentrate the flavours. If you're cooking tomatoes this way, you may as well do a decent amount – I like to have roast tomatoes in the fridge ready to eat with meat and fish. This salad is inspired by the Middle East, with olives purple and beautiful, and the preserved lemon salty and pungent.

At least 4 hours ahead, roast the tomatoes. Heat the oven to 120°C (gas ¼). If you have a convection oven, fine; if not, wedge the door ajar with a wooden spoon, so you can get the air through.

Twist and crumple the bunch of mixed herbs in your hands to release their aromatic oils. Sprinkle half of them over a baking tray with half the salt. Lay the tomatoes cut-side up on top of that, then scatter with the rest of the herbs and salt.

Put the tomatoes in the oven for about 3 hours, until crusty on the outside but still soft on the inside. Remove and leave to cool.

While the tomatoes are roasting, lay the vine leaves on a rack over a roasting tray. Place in the oven for about 30 minutes, until the leaves have dried out. Remove and leave to cool, then cut the leaves into thin strips.

Cut the peel from the preserved lemon, discarding the flesh. Cut the peel into thin strips. In a large bowl, gently combine the roast tomatoes with the strips of vine leaves, preserved lemon peel, olives and both types of parsley.

Mix together all the dressing ingredients and season to taste. Serve the salad and dressing over the top of the carpaccio.

'FRESH GOATS' CHEESE & BEETROOT'

1kg bunch beetroot (about 4),
with leaves

100g green beans

1 tbsp pine nuts

1 tbsp red wine vinegar

2 tbsp extra virgin olive oil

1 garlic clove, crushed

1 tbsp capers, drained and
coarsely chopped

½ tsp cracked black pepper

1 bunch watercress

½ small red onion, finely sliced

200g soft, fresh goats' cheese

This sweet-and-sour combination works really well with the fillet. If your bunch of beetroot does not have leaves, you can substitute baby spinach.

Trim the leaves from the beetroot. Scrub the beetroot and wash the leaves and stems thoroughly. Bring a large saucepan of water to the boil, add the beetroot, then reduce the heat and simmer, covered, for 30 minutes or until tender when pierced with the point of a knife. Drain and leave the beetroot to cool before peeling the skins off and cutting the bulbs into wedges.

Bring another saucepan of water to the boil. Add the beans and cook for 3 minutes or until just tender. Remove the beans with tongs (leave the saucepan on the heat) and plunge them into a bowl of cold water. Drain well.

Add the beetroot leaves and stems to the boiling water and cook for 3-5 minutes, or until tender. Drain, plunge into a bowl of cold water, then leave to drain thoroughly.

To toast the pine nuts, put a heavy-based pan over a high heat and, when it's very hot, turn the heat off and add the pine nuts to the pan. Toss them every 30 seconds or so and, within about 4 minutes, they will be nicely toasted. Remove from the pan and set aside to cool.

Put the vinegar, oil, garlic, capers and pepper in a screw-top jar and shake well. Toss together the beetroot, beans, cooked leaves, watercress, onion, pine nuts, salt, pepper and some dressing. Pile on top of the carpaccio, crumble the goats' cheese over and drizzle with the remaining dressing.

'JAPANESE STYLE WITH TOBIKO'

15g dried wakame, or 70g fresh
   wakame
1 cucumber
3 spring onions
50g enoki mushrooms
10g pickled ginger, chopped
1 handful coriander leaves
about 2 tbsp tobiko
   (flying fish roe)

dressing
50ml dashi broth
50ml dark soy sauce
50ml tamari (sweet soy sauce)
50ml sake
50ml mirin
50g sugar

The wakame used in this salad is lobe-leaf seaweed that can be bought salted or dried. Either way, it needs to be soaked before use, to get rid of the salt or to rehydrate the dried seaweed. If you can find wasabi-flavoured tobiko, use it.

Soak the wakame in water for 20 minutes, rinse then soak again for another 5 minutes. Rinse the seaweed and squeeze it dry.

While the wakame is soaking, peel the cucumber and cut it into julienne. Slice the spring onions across at an angle. Wipe the enoki mushrooms and trim the base of the stalks. Combine the cucumber, spring onions, enoki, pickled ginger and coriander in a bowl and add the prepared seaweed. Toss together gently.

Get out a measuring jug that shows 50ml increments and add each of the dressing ingredients to it in turn. Stir until the sugar dissolves. Mix half the dressing with the salad and leave it to sit for 5 minutes.

Drizzle a tablespoon or so of the remaining dressing over each plate of carpaccio. Put a pile of salad in the centre of each and garnish with a good teaspoon of tobiko.

'ONION RINGS & TOMATO RELISH'

onion rings (page 131)

tomato relish

glug of oil

2 tsp ground cumin

1 tsp ground coriander

1 tsp ground turmeric

1 onion, finely chopped

1 garlic clove

1 can chopped plum tomatoes,
   about 400g

salt and pepper

You can make the tomato relish the day before serving if you like. Heat the oil in a heavy-based pan. Add the spices and fry for 1 minute, then add the onion and cook for a few minutes, stirring constantly, until the onion becomes translucent. Add the garlic and cook for a further minute. Add the chopped tomatoes and bring to the boil. Cook for 10 minutes or until thick, and season well with salt and pepper.

Cook the onion rings according to the recipe on page 131. The best tip I can give you is to peel the onion twice, by which I mean take off the skin and then the next layer too. Big rings, little rings – cook the lot. Whether you serve them with the carpaccio or not is another matter (I always eat them while I'm cooking) but trust me, they will get eaten. Also: always use caution when deep-frying. Never leave the pan unattended, ensure that the handle is not protruding from the stove, and have a tight-fitting lid to hand so you can cover the pan quickly if the oil should set alight.

Lay your carpaccio out on plates. Place a stack of onion rings in the middle and a good spoonful of tomato relish on the side.

'CAPONATA, OLIVE OIL & POACHED EGG'

3 large aubergines
2 long shallots
4 large plum tomatoes
4 sticks celery
200ml olive oil
2 tsp large capers
50g large sultanas
50ml quality red wine vinegar
salt and pepper
50g pine kernels
4 large organic eggs
malt vinegar, for poaching
crusty bread

To me it's important that caponata has a real kick – the sweetness of the dried fruit needs to be offset with a good glug of red wine vinegar. Just as importantly, the texture has to be right: you want soggy aubergines, plump sultanas, and crisp celery for a good caponata.

Remove the calyx from the aubergine (the green bit on top, the same word is used for the green bit of a strawberry – but I digress) and cut the flesh into chunks about the size of your thumb. Chop the shallots, tomatoes and celery to roughly the same size.

Add the oil to a large heavy-based saucepan or casserole and place over medium heat. Add the aubergine and cook slowly, stirring often, for a good 15 minutes or until soft. Take out the aubergines and enough oil should be left to cook the shallots.

Put the shallots in the pan and reduce the heat to low. Gently cook the shallots until clear. Add the tomatoes and continue cooking slowly so they break down to a mush. Return the aubergines to the pan. Add the capers (with a little of their liquid), sultanas, celery and vinegar and cook for a good 20 minutes or so. Season with salt and pepper and stir gently so the mixture doesn't break up too much. The whole thing should smell sweet and sour.

Meanwhile, put a heavy pan over a high heat and let it get really hot. Turn the heat off, add the pine nuts to the pan and leave them to toast in the residual heat, tossing every 30 seconds or so, for about 4 minutes. When nicely browned, remove and set aside.

Poach the eggs in a large pan of gently simmering water with a good amount of malt vinegar. Lift out with a slotted spoon and drain.

Pile the caponata on top of the carpaccio and top each serving with a poached egg. Finish with a drizzle of good-quality olive oil and serve with crusty bread.

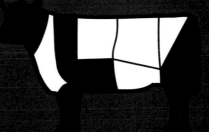

SALADS & SNACKS

Summer days, outside, lunch or dinner, maybe brunch – the salad is a fitting little ensemble for any time. Great salads have a complex taste, but each flavour should be distinct, and there must be a mix of sweet and sour, whether that comes from the dressing, or ingredients like green papaya and beetroot. Texture is paramount – there must be crunch and the soft ooze that comes from a great dressing or well-cooked meat. Both salads and snacks should be moreish – I mean can't-stop-eating-them moreish – but they must not fill you up. They need to leave a clean, crisp flavour lingering as a prelude to the greatness of the next course, or maybe just the next mouthful. I like to make a few dishes and set them out in the middle of the table; it's a great way to eat and they encourage conversation simply by being passed around.

'COLD ROAST BEEF SALAD WITH HORSERADISH, BEETROOT & WATERCRESS'

100g watercress, stripped of the
　big stalks
300g roast beef, thinly sliced
creamed horseradish
8 preserved baby beetroot, cut
　into 4 wedges each
black pepper
olive oil

There are few classic combinations that work as well hot or cold as roast beef, watercress and horseradish. This salad has been created to use up leftover roast beef but it is just as good with a freshly cooked lump of sirloin left to cool to room temperature.

Lay out four large serving plates and drop some watercress on each. Lay some thinly sliced beef over it, and then some more watercress. Now flick the salad with the creamed horseradish. Drop on any remaining beef and scatter the beetroot over. Finish with the last of the watercress and some more creamed horseradish, then a good amount of freshly ground black pepper and a dash of olive oil.

'BLOODY QUICK & EASY THAI BEEF SALAD'

300g trimmed sirloin
a little vegetable oil
100g beansprouts
6 lime leaves, shredded
40g picked Thai basil, or Italian
 basil
30g picked coriander
3 long red chillies, seeds
 removed, cut into thin strips

dressing
juice of 2 limes
25ml vegetable oil
40ml fish sauce
1 long red chilli, finely diced

This is quick-quick-quick and very tasty... great back garden Saturday lunch food, or served as a starter. It's not too hot, so you can always put extra chillies in if that's the way ah-ha ah-ha you like it ah-ha ah-ha.

Cut the beef into thin strips about the length of your little finger. Heat a heavy-based pan over a high heat and leave until very hot. Mix the beef with a little vegetable oil and throw it into the pan. Leave to sizzle for a minute to get colour, then turn and cook for another minute. Remove the meat from the pan and set aside to cool a little.

Toss together the beansprouts, herbs and fine strips of chilli and set to one side.

In a separate bowl, stir together all the dressing ingredients. Pour the dressing over the warm beef, then add the herb salad. Toss well and serve immediately.

'LARP OF BEEF'

400g finely minced beef
30ml fish sauce
90ml lime juice
8 red shallots, sliced
4 tbsp fresh mint
4 tbsp fresh coriander
4 tbsp roasted sticky rice
   (page 58)
1 tsp dried red chilli flakes

to serve
1 long red chilli, finely shredded
1 handful coriander leaves
lettuce leaves and/or betel
   leaves

This is a great salad. In Thailand there would be lots of other things in here, like liver and lung, and the meat would not be cooked at all, but I didn't think that would work here.

Put the beef in a wok or saucepan with a little salted water and simmer for 3 minutes or until the meat is cooked. Take the pan off the heat and let it cool to room temperature, then drain off the excess water.

Just before you want to serve it, add the fish sauce, lime juice, shallots, mint, coriander, roasted rice and chilli flakes. Check that the flavour is hot, salty and sour and add a few extra drops of lime juice if necessary to sharpen and define flavour. Throw the shredded chilli and coriander leaves over the top.

Serve with lettuce leaves and/or betel leaves, using them as edible cups to hold the meat mixture.

'RICE NOODLE & BEEF SALAD WITH MINT & PEANUTS'

400g sirloin
½ tsp freshly ground pepper
1 tsp sesame oil
1 tbsp sugar
2 tbsp Thai fish sauce
200g rice vermicelli
3 Thai shallots, finely sliced
3 garlic cloves, finely sliced
25g mint, chopped
15g Thai basil leaves
15g coriander, chopped
40g snake beans, chopped
150g roasted peanuts, chopped

sauce
1 tbsp rice wine vinegar
4 small red chillies, chopped
130g sugar
2 garlic cloves, crushed
250ml hot water
100ml Thai fish sauce
40ml lime juice
1 small carrot, cut into julienne

A real crowd pleaser, this is an interesting salad because the sauce is used to rehydrate the vermicelli, making them soft and at the same time pumping loads of flavour into what can be very boring noodles. Use more mint and chilli if you like a bigger flavour.

Get a griddle pan seriously hot. Cut the beef into long thin strips and season it with the pepper and sesame oil. Lay the beef strips on the grill and do not touch them until they start to smoke. Turn them and give them another minute. Combine the sugar and fish sauce in a mixing bowl, tip the beef into it and toss well (the fish sauce works in place of salt and gives great flavour when mixed with the charred beef). Leave to cool.

To make the sauce, heat the vinegar in a saucepan. Remove from the heat and add the chillies, sugar, garlic and hot water, then the fish sauce, lime juice, and carrot julienne.

Put the rice vermicelli in a large bowl. Pour the sauce over it and leave until the vermicelli is soft. Drop in the shallots, garlic, herbs and snake beans, then add the beef and mix together. Sprinkle with the chopped nuts, toss and serve.

'SPICED SALAD OF BRAISED BEEF WITH ROAST RICE'

beef

600g sirloin beef trimmings, fat removed

300ml fish sauce

2 litres coconut milk

3 thumb-sized pieces ginger, or some ginger scraps, roughly chopped

1 head galangal, roughly chopped

lemongrass scraps, bruised

10 lime leaves

salad

1 handful white sticky rice

2 green mangoes, peeled and cut into julienne

3 Thai shallots, thinly sliced

2 handfuls picked coriander

1 stalk lemongrass, peeled and sliced into thin rounds

1 large handful Thai basil

1 large handful mint leaves

50ml nam jim dressing (opposite)

This is a complex salad even by my standards, but I have to include it as it has been one of my favourites for about 10 years. I learnt this method of using up the trimmings of beef in the early days of Mezzo. The flavour is intense but the best part is the texture. The meat is stringy but soft, crisp and salty, and with the heat of the chilli and the sourness of the green mango or papaya it is inspired. Master this salad and you will find it hard ever to beat it.

You can store the meat for a few days in the fridge. You can also multiply it as many times as you like for a dinner party or feeding the masses. It is truly addictive, so make loads – it will keep for up to one week. The salad goes really well with Nam Jim dressing opposite.

Put the meat in a large bowl and cover with the fish sauce. Seal with cling film and leave somewhere cool overnight.

Next day, heat the oven to 160°C (gas 3). Remove the beef from the fish sauce and put it in a large roasting pan with the coconut milk, ginger, galangal, lemongrass and lime leaves. Put this in the oven for 1 hour, then raise the temperature to 180°C (gas 4) and continue cooking for a further 40 minutes – check at least once to see how it is going.

Increase the oven temperature again to 220°C (gas 7) and cook for another 40 minutes to caramelize the mixture. It should turn golden brown and most of the milk should evaporate. It will look like the whole thing is burnt but it is not, it's just bloody tasty.

Remove the roasting pan from the oven, and put the meat into a bowl or dish to cool. Do not refrigerate – it is much better served at room temperature – but you can obviously refrigerate any leftovers for the next day.

Meanwhile, soak the rice for the dressing in a bowl of cold water for 10 minutes, then drain well. Spread it out on a baking tray and roast it at 220°C (gas 7), stirring often, until it is lightly browned and smells nutty. Tip into a bowl and leave to cool, then grind to a coarse powder.

To make the salad, put the mangoes, shallots, coriander, lemongrass, basil and mint in a bowl, tearing any very large mint leaves into pieces. Add the dressing and toss gently. Serve the salad and beef together, sprinkling the roasted rice over the top like sesame seeds.

'NAM JIM'

2 large red chillies
2 small green chillies
50g palm sugar
50ml fish sauce
50ml lime juice

This classic recipe is a VIP salad dressing – quick, easy and perfect for all these Thai salads. Make it fresh every time you want to use it.

Dice all the chillies then, using a pestle and mortar, crush them with the palm sugar. Add the fish sauce and lime juice to taste and use as soon as possible, within 6 hours.

'SEARED BEEF FILLET WITH THYME'

12 black peppercorns
½ tbsp sea salt flakes
a few thyme sprigs, leaves
    picked
200g beef fillet
100ml extra virgin olive oil
juice of 1 lemon, plus 4 wedges,
    to serve
2 handfuls mixed leaves, cress
    and salad sprouts
60g pecorino cheese

Grind the peppercorns and mix with the salt and thyme leaves. Rub the fillet lightly with some of the olive oil, then rub the pepper mixture into the beef. Heat a ridged griddle pan until very hot and sear the beef on all sides. Remove from the pan and leave to cool.

Use a long sharp knife to slice the beef as thinly as possible. Place the slices on a board and press along them with the flat side of the knife blade to extend each slice.

Cover your serving plates with the beef. Season, then drizzle over half the lemon juice. Toss the leaves, cress and sprouts with some olive oil and a little more lemon juice. Scatter the leaves over the beef, and then shave the pecorino on top. Drizzle with olive oil and serve with the lemon wedges.

'SEARED SPICED FILLET'

1 tsp ground fennel seed
1 tsp ground coriander
1 tsp ground allspice
1 tsp ground black pepper
1 tsp salt
½ tsp dried chilli flakes
200g centre-cut beef fillet
vegetable oil
pineapple pickle (opposite)

Seared beef is like carpaccio – a very versatile little number. It does need to be paired with strong flavours and, as the crusty coating has things like fennel and chilli, think sweet little chopped tomatoes mixed with coriander and a little ginger. Have fun.

Combine the ground spices, salt and chilli flakes and spread them out on a plate. Heat a skillet or a very heavy frying pan until really hot (you shouldn't be able to hold your hand over it).

Take the beef and roll it in the spice mix. Once this is done, you must sear it as quickly as possible. Pour a little oil into the pan and add the beef. Move it quickly so the spices do not burn but the beef starts to colour. It takes about 20 seconds on each side and around 2 minutes in total.

Remove the beef from the pan. Wrap it up in cling film, sealing the ends like a sausage, then chill. When ready to serve, slice the beef very thinly and serve it with the pineapple pickle (opposite) on the side.

'PINEAPPLE PICKLE'

Makes about 700g

½ pineapple
3 fresh green chillies
255ml vegetable oil
3 cloves
2 star anise
2 small cinnamon sticks
2 sprigs curry leaves, leaves
   picked
100g caster or granulated sugar
salt

(a)

1 tsp coriander seeds
1 tsp fennel seeds
1 tsp cumin seeds

(b)

10 dried chillies, soaked in warm
   water for 15 minutes
1 thumb-sized piece fresh young
   turmeric, peeled

(c)

8 small Thai shallots, chopped
5 garlic cloves

Making the pineapple pickle is like being at school. Add (a) to (b) and it equals wow!

Grind (a), (b) and (c) separately until fine.

Remove the skin, eyes and core of the pineapple and cut the flesh into bite-sized triangles. Cut the chillies into 1.5cm strips and set them aside with the pineapple.

Heat a frying pan and add the oil. When it is very hot, add (c) and stir for 1 minute. Then add (a) and (b), plus the cloves, star anise and cinnamon. Stir well, until the mixture is fragrant.

Add the pineapple, green chillies, curry leaves, sugar and salt to taste. Reduce the heat and cook, stirring, until the pineapple pieces are soft. Simmer for 1 hour. Do not add water during cooking as this will dilute the taste. Allow to cool then serve. You can store the leftovers in a jar in the fridge for up to 1 month.

'GRILLED BEEF WITH THAI FLAVOURS IN RICE PAPER'

400g beef skirt, trimmed
a little vegetable oil
50g beansprouts
1 large carrot, shredded
1 handful coriander
1 handful torn mint leaves
1 handful basil
nam jim dressing (page 59)
24-32 rice paper wrappers

marinade

1 stick lemongrass
1 garlic clove, finely chopped
1 shallot, finely chopped
1 bird's-eye chilli, finely
   chopped
1 tsp fish sauce
1 tsp lime juice
1 tsp water
1 tsp toasted sesame oil
2 tsp toasted sesame seeds

This takes two days to make because it uses beef skirt. The beef is tough unless it is left to break down in a marinade, but if you persist it will be well worth it. Go on: drop it in the marinade on Thursday and cook for dinner Saturday. If you really fancy it tonight, buy a good piece of sirloin; the recipe will still work but you will lose the intensity of flavour from the two-days of marinating. Dress it with the nam jim (page 59).

Slice the beef into strips roughly the size of your finger, cutting the meat against the grain.

Using a mortar and pestle, or a food processor, grind all the marinade ingredients together to make a paste. Coat the beef in the marinade and leave covered in a non-plastic container for 2 days to tenderize.

When ready to cook, heat a griddle pan. Add a little oil and drop the marinated beef on the griddle, cooking it fast and hard so that it is charred outside and a little pink in the middle. Remove from the heat and, using a really sharp knife, slice the meat into the thinnest strips you can.

Mix together the vegetables and herbs. Sprinkle with a little nam jim dressing and stir.

Working with one rice paper wrapper at a time, dip them in a dish of cool water for 30 seconds to 1 minute, then lay them on a tea towel to help absorb the excess water. Pile on some of the veg with as much beef as you like down the middle, then roll them up. (The tip is if you roll them and they are so big they don't fit in your mouth you have put too much in!)

Repeat using the rest of the ingredients and serve with the remaining nam jim dressing as a dipping sauce.

'THAI SATAY WITH PEANUT SAUCE'

peanut sauce
50ml vegetable oil
1 shallot, finely chopped
1 tbsp Thai red curry paste
2 small red chillies, seeds
   removed, finely chopped
300g freshly ground peanuts,
   or crunchy peanut butter
50ml soy sauce
1 large handful chopped
   coriander

satay beef
500g rump or sirloin
100ml light soy sauce
200ml mirin
100g miso paste

The main vegetable market in Bangkok is Phat Klong Talat, which opens at 4am. Street sellers set up to provide the traders and customers with breakfast. As you approach the stalls the smell is intoxicating. The best satay I have ever eaten came off some long metal guttering filled with hot charcoal and covered with wire. This recipe is inspired by those great market sellers who could feed me satay for breakfast any day. The sauce works just as well with fish or chicken.

Start with the peanut sauce. Heat the oil in a saucepan over a moderate heat. Add the shallot and fry gently for 3 minutes. Add the curry paste and chillies and cook, stirring constantly, for 5 minutes until the paste is fragrant. Mix in the peanuts (or peanut butter) and 200ml water, and bring to the boil, stirring well. Stir in the soy sauce, then remove from the heat and leave to cool.

Meanwhile, soak 24 bamboo skewers in warm water for about an hour. This makes it easier to thread the meat and prevents the wood burning while the meat cooks, especially over coals.

To make the satay, cut the beef into thin strips approximately 4cm long, 1cm wide and 0.5cm thick. In a bowl, mix together the soy, mirin and miso, then stir in the strips of meat. Leave to marinate for 20 minutes.

Thread the meat on the skewers ensuring the maximum amount of meat is exposed so that it cooks quickly and stays moist and tender when placed over the coals. Grill the satay, preferably over coals, otherwise on a very hot griddle plate. Turn the sticks over every 30 seconds or so – a good satay will only take a couple of minutes to cook if the coals or griddle are hot enough.

Once the peanut sauce is cool, stir in the coriander and serve as a dipping sauce for the satay.

'FRAGRANT SATAY WITH PEANUT & COCONUT SAUCE'

Soak 20 bamboo skewers in warm water for an hour. Cut the meat into strips about the size of your little finger (unless you have a huge little finger, then think of a delicate little finger!). Drop the meat into a bowl with the light soy sauce and sesame oil and leave for a while, preferably an hour. Thread the meat on the skewers and refrigerate.

Meanwhile, in a saucepan, combine the coconut cream and red curry paste and cook for 5 minutes over a low heat – the mixture should become fragrant as the spices cook. Add the sugar and a shake of fish sauce, give it a good stir, then add the peanut butter.

Bring the sauce to the boil. Add the coconut milk, then return to the boil and taste. It should be spicy but not too hot, and it should be thick –more like peanut custard than porridge.

Grill the satay, preferably over coals, otherwise on a very hot griddle plate. Sprinkle the satay with a little oil and sit the ends that have no meat over the edge so you can turn them easily. They need to cook quick and fast so heat, heat and more heat. Turn them every 30 seconds or so – a good satay will only take a couple of minutes to cook if the coals or griddle are hot enough. Each one should have a slightly crisp exterior but be pink inside.

Serve with the peanut sauce on the side, scattered with coriander.

500g beef rib or rump, something with a little fat in it
50ml light soy sauce
1 tsp sesame oil
100g coconut cream
2 tbsp red curry paste
3 tbsp palm sugar or brown sugar
a little fish sauce
150g chunky peanut butter
1 x 400g can coconut milk
1 handful chopped fresh coriander

'BEEF IN BLACK BEANS & CORIANDER'

300g beef sirloin

2 garlic cloves

4 coriander roots or stems

1 knob ginger, peeled

60ml vegetable oil

50ml sherry

1 tsp sesame oil

4 spring onions, sliced, white
and green separated

1-2 tbsp black bean sauce

to serve

300g ho fung noodles, or boiled
rice

2 handfuls coriander leaves

Beef in black bean sauce is one of those Chinese classics that can sometimes be really flavourless but the paste of garlic and ginger adds real depth of flavour to this number.

Cut the beef as thinly as possible into long slices, then cut the slices into strips. They need to be long and thin so that when the beef is cooked it mounds like spaghetti with a sauce. Use a mortar and pestle to pound together the garlic, coriander roots or stems and the ginger.

Heat a wok and, when it is hot, pour in the oil. Add the garlic-ginger paste, stir and cook for a minute – the flavours will really get up your nose and give off a strangely bubble gum-like smell. Add the beef, increase the heat and stir-fry for a minute. Add the sherry and sesame oil, and stir-fry until the beef is coloured. Throw in the whites of the spring onions and the black bean sauce, and stir-fry for 3 minutes.

Serve with noodles or rice, or whatever you like, sprinkling the coriander and the green parts of the spring onions over the top.

'KOFTAS, PEPPERS AND TZATZIKI'

2 tsp cumin seeds

2 tbsp coriander seeds

500g minced beef

juice of 2 lemons

1 large handful mint, chopped

40g pine nuts, toasted

salt and pepper

1 large egg, lightly beaten

6 red peppers

olive oil

1 garlic clove, peeled

150ml plain yoghurt

I'm still an Aussie at heart and reckon you can't beat cooking in the great outdoors with barbecues and mates and beer and falafels and kebabs and dips and stuff. All three of the recipes here can be served in their own right but work even better together. Although peppers aren't that seasonal, they work well with the combination. Serve with Turkish flatbread or warm naan.

Heat the oven to 220°C (gas 7). Put a heavy-based pan without oil over a high heat. Once it is hot, take it off the heat and add the cumin and coriander seeds. Let them toast without any further heat for 2-3 minutes, until they change colour and release their fragrance. Crush them with a pestle and mortar and set aside.

Put the beef mince into a bowl. Stir in half the lemon juice, 4 tbsp of mint, the pine nuts and crushed spices. Season well with salt and pepper, then bind the mixture with the egg. Shape into ten little balls and put them in the fridge for a good 30 minutes.

Put the peppers on a baking tray, rub with a little olive oil and roast until dark. Take out, drop into a big bowl and cover with cling film to help the skin to blister. Leave for 10 minutes. Peel off the skins, discard the cores and seeds, and cut the flesh into hunks – quarters are good. Mix the juices left in the bowl with the remaining lemon juice. Season and taste, then add a dash of olive oil if needed. Drop the peeled peppers into this dressing and leave. They will last a good 2 days in the fridge so can be done well before serving.

Heat 3 tablespoons olive oil in a frying pan until fairly hot. Fry the koftas for 6-7 minutes, turning occasionally, until they are golden brown and cooked through.

To make the tzatziki, use a pestle and mortar to crush the garlic to a paste with a little salt. Put the yoghurt in a small bowl, stir in the garlic paste and remaining mint and you are ready to serve.

'ĆEVAPČIĆI'

700g lean beef mince
454g lamb mince
350g pork mince
20g onion, very finely chopped
3 medium garlic cloves, crushed
1 tbsp bicarbonate of soda
4 tsp salt
2½ tsp hot paprika (Hungarian
   if possible)
black pepper
olive oil

The Vineyard in St Kilda, Melbourne, was a restaurant that specialized in steak, and during my teenage years was a huge inspiration to me. It was owned by the man who ran the local Yugoslavian football team, and one of the dishes it served as a starter was ćevapčići (Yugoslavian sausage) with whole red peppers in their own juices. It was absolutely delicious. I was shown how to make cevapčići in my fourth year as an apprentice by a very bling Yugoslavian who prided himself on his dress but more importantly his food.

The main ingredients were beef mince, bicarbonate of soda, hot paprika and garlic, lots and lots of garlic.

Mix the meat, onions, garlic, bicarbonate of soda, salt, hot paprika, and some pepper together in a large bowl.

To form the ćevaps traditionally, moisten your hands with olive oil and shape the paste into long rolls about 2.5cm x 7.5cm – you'll have around 25 to 30 of them. Fry or grill the rolls, preferably over hot coals, and eat them straight away.

'ANCHOVY, FONTINA & MEAT SAUCE CALZONE'

dough
250ml tepid water
50ml olive oil
15g honey
15g fresh yeast
10g salt
250g plain flour

filling
150g fontina cheese, grated
100g canned anchovies, drained
200ml meat sauce (page 80)

I love these little parcels filled with cheese and meat and stuff – they are very moreish.

Combine the tepid water, olive oil, honey, yeast, salt and two pinches of flour in a saucepan and place over low heat to dissolve – it should start to bubble in about 5 minutes. Put the rest of the flour in a bowl and pour the liquid ingredients into it, mixing to form a dough. Knead by hand for about 10 minutes (it's good exercise) or knead it in a machine for 5 minutes, until the dough is silky and strong.

Put the dough in a bowl, cover with cling film and leave somewhere warm. It will take about 40 minutes to double in size. Meanwhile, prepare the filling ingredients.

When the dough is ready, take the risen dough and punch it down (this is called knocking back, although it's quite different from a shot of tequila). Heat the oven to 240-250°C (gas 9-10).

Roll the dough into a sausage shape and then cut it into ten equal pieces. Roll each one out into a circle and divide the cheese, anchovies and meat sauce between them, piling them in the middle. Brush the edges with a little warm water, then fold one side of each dough circle over to give a half-moon shape and press to seal the edges.

Put the calzone on a baking sheet and bake for 10-15 minutes or until they are nicely coloured. Remove from the oven and serve hot or at room temperature.

'OMELETTE WITH ASIAN GREENS, GINGERED BEEF & GARLIC'

filling

125ml vegetable oil

5cm ginger, peeled and finely sliced

2 garlic cloves, crushed

200g minced beef

125g green bok choy, leaves separated

125g white bok choy, leaves separated

200g choy sum, leaves separated

2 tsp sesame oil

½ cucumber, thinly sliced lengthways

4 tbsp fish sauce

omelette

5 medium eggs, lightly beaten

fish sauce

4 tbsp vegetable oil

Tip Ideally you would slice the cucumber using a mandolin. Whether you have one of the expensive metal models or a cheap Japanese plastic one, watch your fingers. If you don't have a mandolin, use a vegetable peeler to cut the cucumber into thin strips.

Thai omelettes (which are really deep-fried, flavoured egg pancakes filled with almost anything) are one of my favourite-ever eats. This one is a two-stager because you have to make the filling. I know it sounds like a lot of work, but it is so good to eat you will do it more than once – and I believe you could charge people who come round for dinner, it is so worthwhile.

Start with the filling. Heat the oil in a wok over a high heat. Add the ginger and garlic and cook for 1 minute, then add the mince and fry for 2 minutes, until browned but not dry. Add the mixed greens and toss for 3-4 minutes, until wilted, then add the sesame oil and cucumber and cook for a further 3 minutes, stirring well. Remove from the heat, stir in the fish sauce and set aside.

To make the omelette, lightly beat the eggs together in a bowl and season with a little fish sauce. Heat a clean wok over a medium heat and add the oil, tilting the pan to ensure it is evenly coated. Pour in the eggs and roll around until the surface of the pan is covered, using the back of a spoon to spread the omelette evenly. Once a skin has formed, allow it to cook, still tilting and smoothing, for 3-4 minutes, then lift the omelette out of the pan and place it on a clean tea towel. At this stage the top of the omelette will still be liquid, but it will continue cooking as it cools.

Lay the filling across the omelette and, using the tea towel, lift one edge over the greens. Continue rolling the omelette as though you were making a Swiss roll, so that the greens are securely enclosed. Cut the omelette roll across at an angle into four pieces and place them on serving plates. Serve immediately, with extra fish sauce for seasoning.

'KOBEBA WITH GROUND RICE'

shell
250g lean minced beef
300g ground rice
salt and pepper
about 6 tbsp water

filling
350g minced beef
1 medium onion, grated
½ tsp allspice
1 tsp ground cinnamon

Like most other Australians, I grew up with a mix of culinary influences. Recipes such as these traditional Mediterranean dumplings filtered down to us from the food served in restaurants. It's important that the meat be very lean, or the dumplings can fall apart.

To make the shell, put the meat, ground rice, and ½ teaspoon salt into a food processor and whiz thoroughly. Add just enough water to produce a soft, dryish paste that holds together well.

Next prepare the filling by working all the filling ingredients together, with some salt and pepper, by hand until a paste forms.

When making the dumplings, some people like to wet their hands with water so that the paste does not stick, others flour them, and some oil them. Take lumps of the ground rice and meat paste, a little smaller than a walnut, and roll them into balls. Make a dent in the middle of each dumpling with your finger, then pinch the sides and lift them up as though you were shaping a pot, making the shell as thin as possible.

Stuff with 1 teaspoon of filling then bring the sides of the shell up over the filling, pinching the edges together to close the dumplings. Roll lightly into a ball.

Variations There are many ways you can change the flavouring of the filling, such as adding finely chopped flat-leaf parsley or celery leaves. In Iraq the filling has parsley or celery leaves, plus ½ teaspoon ground cardamom, or 1 teaspoon pulverized dried limes, while in Calcutta the filling would be flavoured with ginger, garlic, turmeric and chopped fresh coriander.

Although many people deep-fry their kobeba in oil before stewing them, to give them a golden colour and make them firm, some people now roast them briefly first in a hot oven. I simply poach mine in stock or a stew for about 25 minutes.

'PELMENI'

dumpling dough
80ml milk or water
1 egg
salt
350g plain flour

filling
250g beef fillet trimmings
2 small onions
1 garlic clove
5 drops olive oil
1 handful chopped parsley

to serve
150g soured cream
1 large handful dill, torn

My uncle's mother, Nanna Hinki, taught me to make these Russian dumplings when I was about eight. The filling needs to be smooth. You must chop the beef and the onions very, very finely so that they are almost a paste. The mixture should be sandy when cooked, at which point the oil is beaten into it.

Put the milk or water in a saucepan, bring to the boil, then add the egg and a pinch of salt and mix them together. Pour this mixture into the flour and mix into a dough. Set aside to rest for about 40 minutes.

Chop the beef trimmings by hand until fine and even, then chop the onions so that they too are very fine. Make a smooth paste of the garlic with ½ teaspoon of salt. Now mix all the filling ingredients together in a large bowl and beat it and beat it and beat it into as fine a paste as you can.

Roll the dough out until it is 1.5-2mm thick. Using a 6cm-diameter cookie cutter or glass, cut out rounds. Place one little ball of the filling in the centre of each dough round, then fold the dough over to make semi-circles. Take the corners of each semi-circle, curl them around your finger and pinch together to seal – as though you were making tortellini or fortune cookies.

Drop the dumplings gently in to slightly salty boiling water and wait until the water boils, then leave them for about 7-10 minutes. When the pelmeni rise to the top, they are ready to be taken out with a slotted spoon. Remember to let the water drain away before you put them onto the plate

To serve, toss with the soured cream and torn fresh dill.

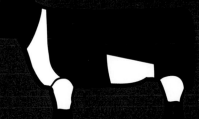

PASTA & RICE

Bolognese or meat sauce or ragu is a godsend to anyone who has kids. I reckon more of it is eaten in my house than any other single dish. It goes on spaghetti, on toast, in toasted sandwiches, in cannelloni, under mash and into Jessie's (my missus's) famous and very, very good lasagne. The sauce recipes here make loads so you'll have leftovers ready for putting in the freezer – cooking enough for more than one meal is something I think we should all be doing more of, rather than worrying about cooking quick dishes every day. For the mince – glorious mince – you need something with a good blend of fat and lean meat. The best formula will be something like 40 per cent fat – yes truly that much! – otherwise it will not be moist. Most mince cooks quickly and without the fat it will turn grainy and sandy.

'MEAT SAUCE'

Makes about 2 litres

1kg beef shin and/or skirt or ox cheek, cut into hand-sized chunks

salt and pepper

2 carrots

2 leeks

2 celery sticks

2 bay leaves

1 small bunch flat-leaf parsley, plus extra chopped parsley for serving

1 small bunch sage

about 6 tbsp olive oil

200g thickly sliced bacon, cut into large chunks

2 x 400g cans chopped tomatoes

375ml red wine

I like this sauce really sticky, thick and gooey. Using two forks to pull the meat apart is a classic technique: just dig in and pull – it works wonders.

Heat the oven to 190°C (gas 5). Season the beef really well. Tie the carrots, leek, celery and herbs together tightly in a bundle.

Heat the olive oil in a large, heavy casserole. Add the bacon and cook for 2 minutes, then add the beef. Wait until the chunks are well browned underneath, then turn them over and cook for a further 10 minutes, making sure to turn the bacon too (if it seems to be browning too quickly, you can always take it out and return it to the sauce at the next step).

Add the bundle of veg and herbs. Pour in the tomatoes and wine and bring to the boil. Let it bubble away for about 10 minutes, scraping the sticky bits of meat from the bottom of the pan.

Pour in a litre or so of water, enough so that it almost covers the meat. Put the lid on and transfer to the oven for an hour to continue cooking. Take the lid off, give the sauce a good stir, then pop it back in the oven to cook for another hour so that much of the liquid can evaporate. Remove the casserole from the oven and leave the sauce to cool for half an hour or so.

Shred the meat well using two forks to pull it apart. Chop the vegetables finely, discarding the herbs. Return the meat and vegetables to the casserole. If the sauce is soupy, bring it to the boil to get rid of some of the liquid but remember this will be served with pasta or bread so it doesn't want to be dry. Taste and adjust the seasoning as necessary. (At this point you could let some of the sauce cool and store it in Ziploc bags in the freezer.)

Chop up a load of parsley and fold it through the sauce only just before serving so that the parsley stays nice and green.

'RICHARD & JUDY'S SPAGHETTI BOLOGNESE'

500g lean minced beef
olive oil
1 packet chicken livers
1 large or 2 medium onions
4 cloves crushed garlic
2 large tins chopped tomatoes
a good squirt of tomato purée
2 Oxo cubes
generous handful mixed herbs
most of a bottle of decent red
   wine, Merlot for choice
seasoning
1 glass amontillado sherry
parmesan cheese

For many years I worked on 'This Morning', a magazine programme with Richard Madeley and Judy Finnegan. What an awesome TV couple! They always boasted that their spaghetti bolognese recipe was by far the best. Well, time for you to judge! I have to say it's pretty good – as you can imagine, I have eaten it a few times; better when made by Judy than by Richard!!

Brown off the mince in a large, deep frying pan with a little olive oil.

Ditto chicken livers.

Put meat to one side and place well-chopped onion into pan.

Stir on medium heat until soft.

Stir in crushed garlic. Do not brown it.

Add mince, chicken livers, chopped tomatoes, purée, Oxo, herbs, wine.

Bring to boil, stirring occasionally, then reduce to simmer.

Simmer for 90 minutes, stirring occasionally. Add more wine or water if necessary. After 90 minutes, season to taste and add sherry.

Serve 5 minutes later on bed of spaghetti with freshly grated parmesan.

'MY MEAT RAGU'

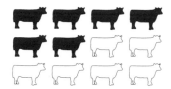

1kg minced beef

200ml red wine

60ml vegetable or olive oil

2 large onions, diced

2 garlic cloves, crushed

salt and pepper

3 bay leaves

a good shake of dried herbs,
     such as oregano or thyme, but
     not a lot

3 x 400g cans plum tomatoes

20g tomato paste, about ½ tube

Someone, somewhere will say this is wrong but this is how I do it! I learned this at age eight, from an Italian. Try to avoid supermarket mince as it is frozen before mincing in huge quantities, and it cooks like chicken pellets. Instead buy mince from a good butcher. A good ragu needs fat to keep it moist and full flavoured. Make lots and store it in the freezer for a rainy day.

Take the meat and massage the red wine into it so that the mince absorbs it. Heat a big, heavy pan. Add the oil and onions and cook gently (or sweat) until the onions are translucent. Add the garlic, a good amount of ground pepper and a teaspoon of salt. Stir and stir until the garlic starts to give off a fragrant aroma.

Add the meat and herbs, and continue cooking and stirring for a few minutes, until the meat starts to get a little colour. Add the canned tomatoes and tomato paste, and bring to the boil. Turn the heat down to a simmer and cook for 2 hours, stirring every half an hour or so. Taste and adjust the seasoning as necessary, then serve with any pasta or gnocchi (recipes on pages 85-87).

'GNOCCHI ALLA ROMANA'

500ml milk
1 garlic clove, crushed
salt and pepper
250g semolina
100g parmesan cheese, grated
100g pecorino cheese, grated
2 egg yolks
about 150g butter
oil, for greasing
2 balls mozzarella cheese
1 handful chopped sage
meat sauce (pages 80-82)

I've given you three types of meat sauce, and here I'm giving you two types of gnocchi. They are interchangeable and really bloody delicious. Gnocchi alla Romana are usually baked in little ovenproof dishes with the sauce spooned over.

In a large saucepan, heat the milk to scalding point with the garlic and some black pepper. Add the semolina and cook, stirring, until it thickens – it should be the same consistency as porridge. Take the pan from the heat and stir in the parmesan and pecorino, really beating the mixture with a wooden spoon to get some air into it. When the mixture has cooled a little, beat in the egg yolks, 50g butter and some salt and pepper.

Lightly oil a baking tray and pour the semolina into it so it's about the thickness of your finger. Leave to cool in the fridge for a few hours or overnight.

When the semolina has set, heat the oven to 220-240°C (gas 7-9). Using a pastry cutter or a large glass, cut it into discs. Butter the inside of ten individual ovenproof dishes (or one large one) really well. Lay the semolina discs in the dish(es). Rub the tops with some more butter and bake for 10 minutes. They should puff up and turn golden.

Take the dishes from the oven. Now you can either tear up the mozzarella, scatter it over the gnocchi and bake for another 5 minutes until the cheese melts, then serve with your meat sauce, or spoon the meat sauce over the gnocchi then cover with cheese and return to the oven for 5 minutes. Sprinkle with chopped sage before serving.

'POTATO GNOCCHI'

1kg floury potatoes
500g plain flour
salt
butter
meat sauce (pages 80-82)
parmesan or fontina cheese,
  grated

Peel the potatoes and boil them in a small amount of water. Drain off all the water then cover the top of the pot with a tea towel and place the lid on the pot – this will help absorb the excess water so the mash will be fluffy. After 5 minutes take off the lid and the towel and mash, mash, mash.

Pour the mashed potato onto a chopping board, add the flour and some salt and knead to a dough while warm. It is ready when the dough comes away from your hands like plasticine.

Roll the dough into a sausage shape 2cm wide and as long as you can. Cut it into 3cm-long lozenges or pieces, or little sausages or whatever you want to call them. Roll each one over the back of a fork to get some grooves in it.

Get a big pot full of water boiling and drop the gnocchi into the water a good handful at a time. They should float to the surface then simmer (if they boil they will break up) for 3 minutes. Lift them out of the water with a slotted spoon and drop them into a bowl with some olive oil. You can do this the day before serving.

Arrange the gnocchi in a buttered dish and pour over some meat sauce. Sprinkle with grated parmesan or fontina cheese and bake for 10 minutes so the dish is seriously hot.

'PASTA'

500g oo flour, plus extra for
  dusting
salt
4 whole eggs, plus 3 egg yolks
1 tbsp olive oil

I know there are plenty of great products on the market and lots of people can't be bothered to make pasta at home – but it is very satisfying once you know the basics, and it allows you to make all sorts of parcels and shapes with whatever fillings you like. Use oo or 'doppio zero' flour as softer flours absorb too much liquid and the resulting pasta is just not strong enough. The recipe here makes about 600g dough, enough for four to six good-sized ravioli for four people.

Put the flour and a pinch of salt into a food processor. Add half the eggs and half the extra yolks and mix until incorporated. Add the oil and whiz again.

In a mixing jug, beat together the rest of the eggs and yolks and start adding them to the processor a little at a time. Stop and feel the texture of the mixture regularly. When it is ready, it will be like large loose breadcrumbs that hold together as dough if you squeeze them between your fingertips. You may not need to use all the eggs – you may even need to add a little more.

Tip the mixture out on to a floured work surface and push it together, then knead until it forms a dough. Wrap in cling film and leave to rest for several hours before use. Roll out on a pasta machine following the manufacturer's instructions and cut into the desired shape.

'OXTAIL RAVIOLI WITH SOY & GINGER BROTH'

oxtail

1 large oxtail, in chunks
salt and pepper
60g plain flour
60ml vegetable oil
1 large carrot, peeled and diced
1 onion, diced
½ celery stick, diced
1 garlic clove, crushed
1 knob galangal or ginger,
  peeled and crushed
50g butter
100ml port
200ml red wine
about 400ml beef stock
  (page 22)
30ml dark soy sauce
2 tsp fish sauce
1 star anise

pasta

600g fresh pasta dough
  (page 87)
1 egg, beaten
salt
1 splash olive oil

This recipe is seriously cheffy and I know that many of you will not want to make it, but the braised oxtail is gorgeous and it could simply be tossed with a few noodles and people would love it. However, if you do make the ravioli, it will be fun, and it's a good dish for getting the kids involved. The broth is also good served over noodles with some shredded vegetables and spring onions, and maybe an egg.

Take a big cast-iron casserole and place it over a high heat. Turn the oven on to 180°C (gas 4). Trim the excess fat from the oxtail. Season it well, then roll it in the flour. Heat the vegetable oil in the casserole and fry the oxtail until well browned.

Take the meat out and set aside. Add the vegetables, garlic and galangal or ginger to the casserole, plus the butter, and cook until the vegetables are well browned, stirring all the time to scrape up the brown bits from the bottom of the pan. Pour in the port and boil until half the liquid has evaporated, then add the wine and do the same.

Drop the oxtail back into the pot and stir quickly to coat with the sauce. Combine the stock, soy sauce, fish sauce and star anise and pour the mixture over the oxtail (there should be enough liquid to cover, if not add more stock). Stir well, then cover and transfer the casserole to the oven. Do not touch it for an hour and a half, then take the lid off and cook for a further hour.

When the meat is done, lift the oxtail from the sauce and strip the meat from it. Strain the sauce, setting the vegetables aside and returning the sauce to the pot. Bring to the boil and keep boiling to reduce the sauce to a sticky syrup. In a bowl, mash the meat, then stir in the vegetables and a little sauce to give a stiff mixture that can be used to fill ravioli or tortellini.

Working in batches as necessary, put the pasta dough through a pasta machine, or use a rolling pin to roll it out to sheets about 1mm thick. Work as quickly as you can as the more the pasta dries out, the more it will lose its elasticity. While you are rolling each batch, keep the remainder moist by wrapping it in cling film. Cut the dough into circles about 7cm in diameter and keep them wrapped in cling film until you are ready to fill them.

Lay half the circles out on the worktop. Place a little of the meat mixture in the centre of each and brush the edges of the dough with egg. Lay the remaining pasta circles over the top and pinch well all around the edges to seal.

To make the broth, put all the ingredients in a large saucepan, bring to the boil and cook for 3 minutes. Leave to infuse on the side of the stove until you are ready to serve.

Bring a large pot of salted water to a rolling boil, adding a drop of olive oil. If you don't have a large pot, it is better to cook the ravioli in batches in separate pans than try to cram too many into one pan. Add the ravioli: they will gradually float to the surface and will be ready 2 minutes after that (so about 4 minutes of cooking in all).

Meanwhile, strain the broth, discarding the solids, and reheat it. Do not let it come to the boil again or it will turn bitter. Drain the ravioli well and place one in each serving bowl. Sprinkle in some spring onions and chillies, then pour the broth over and serve immediately.

broth
400ml beef stock
1 tsp fish sauce
1 knob ginger, crushed
2 star anise
3 coriander roots
1 tbsp dark soy sauce

garnish
2 spring onions, sliced
  diagonally
2 red chillies, sliced diagonally,
  seeds removed if desired

Pasta & Rice   **89**

Variation: Veal & Spinach Meatballs
Take about 400g spinach leaves and wilt
them in a saucepan using only the water
that's left clinging to them after washing.
Drain well and, once cool, squeeze the excess
water out with your hands so the spinach is
really dry. Put it in a food processor with
200g minced veal, 2 slices of bread that
you've soaked in a little water and squeezed
dry, 2 eggs, plus some salt, pepper and
½ teaspoon grated nutmeg. Blend to a paste.
Shape the mixture into balls then roll them
in flour and fry in vegetable oil, turning until
brown on all sides.

'SPAGHETTI AND MEATBALLS'

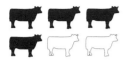

150ml olive oil
2 large onions, finely chopped
salt and pepper
200g fresh breadcrumbs
1kg beef mince
1 handful chopped parsley, or
  some other herbs if you like
200-250ml red wine
6 large fresh tomatoes, chopped
2 x 400g cans chopped tomatoes
500g dried spaghetti
parmesan cheese, grated

This is a dish that should really be served out of the big cooking pot on the table. It needs to slop, drip and splatter. It has to be piping hot and soaked with sauce, and sprinkled with freshly grated parmesan. A 500g pack of spaghetti will be fine for four to six people as long as you have lots of meatballs. Now look: everybody loves meatballs so make LOADS. That is my best advice, my friend.

Put the olive oil in a heavy casserole. Add the onions, plenty of black pepper, and some salt. Turn the heat to medium and cook the onions slowly until soft, but not coloured.

Put 200ml water in a large bowl. Add half the cooked onions and the breadcrumbs. Take the casserole off the heat, then lift out the rest of the onions, leaving as much oil as possible in the pan, and set them aside separately for the sauce. Add the mince, chopped parsley and lots of seasoning to the breadcrumb mixture. Mix until the whole thing becomes a paste, then shape into balls about the size of a ping-pong ball.

Put the casserole over a high heat, add the meatballs and cook for a good 10 minutes before gently turning them and continuing to cook until they are brown. Take them out and add the reserved cooked onions to the pot along with the wine. As it boils, scrape all the brown bits off the base of the pan.

Add the fresh tomatoes and stir over a high heat until they start to break down. Add the canned tomatoes and a can full of water, bring to the boil and cook for 5 minutes. Put the meatballs back in the pan, return to the boil, then simmer for 15 minutes.

Meanwhile, cook the spaghetti and grate the cheese. I like to put the whole lot together in the casserole for serving, but many don't, so it's your choice.

'RISOTTO WITH WILD GARLIC'

45g butter
1 tbsp olive oil
2 small shallots, diced
4 garlic cloves, crushed
900ml beef stock
350g arborio rice
100g parmesan cheese, grated
1 good handful of wild garlic
  leaves, torn

Here is a basic recipe to which you can add whatever you like – the rule is that ingredients that need to cook go in at the beginning; while herbs, leaves and cooked ingredients are added at the end. Wild garlic leaves are around for a short period only in good markets (ask your fruit and vegetable man to get some for you). Be careful, though, as they are a lot stronger than they look. If you can't get them, try a mix of soft herbs, such as sage, basil, chives and chervil, thrown in at the last minute.

Heat 15g butter and the oil in a large, heavy-bottomed pan. Add the shallots and cook until just translucent, then add the garlic and cook for another 3-4 minutes. Put the stock in a separate saucepan and bring it to the boil. Add the rice to the onions and stir around for a couple of minutes to coat the grains and stop them sticking together.

Your pot of boiling stock should be at the ready. It is important that the stock and rice are of a similar temperature, so that the heat doesn't fall when you add the stock to the pan. If it does, the rice may not rehydrate properly, which will result in it being cooked on the outside while remaining quite hard on the inside. Add a couple of ladles of stock and stir around with a spatula until all the liquid is taken up and the rice can be scraped from the bottom of the pan.

Keep adding stock, stirring and scraping all the time, to avoid sticking. After about 15-20 minutes the grains will be tender but still firm to the bite and the risotto will be creamy and moist. Add the parmesan and the remaining butter and whip with a wooden spoon to put more air into the now-creamy rice. Throw in the torn wild garlic leaves and serve immediately.

'WILD MUSHROOM & TRUFFLE RISOTTO'

400ml beef stock (page 22)
100g portobello mushrooms,
   sliced
60ml olive oil
2 shallots, diced
1 garlic clove, crushed to a paste
100g wild mushrooms, cleaned
   and trimmed
salt and pepper
150g Vialone Nano rice
40g parmesan cheese, grated
20g butter, diced
1 handful chopped parsley
1 small truffle, scrubbed
20ml truffle oil

This is good hearty food that goes down well with most generations on most occasions.

Bring the stock to the boil in a large saucepan, then turn it off, drop in the portobello mushrooms and stir.

In another wide saucepan, heat the oil and fry the shallots slowly, without letting them brown. When they look softish, add the garlic (it will burn if you put it in at the same time as the shallots). Drop in the wild mushrooms, season with a tiny amount of salt but lots of black pepper, and cook, stirring, for 1 minute. Remove the mushroom mixture from the pan, leaving behind as much oil as possible, and set aside.

Add the rice to the pan and stir quickly in one direction only, keeping the heat high. The rice will take up the oil. Although this is not a difficult dish, it's worth taking it steady. Start to ladle the stock and mushrooms into the pan of rice. Stir until all the stock has been absorbed, then add another ladle of stock and stir again. Keep going until all the stock is used or the rice is cooked, whichever happens first. For me the rice should be cooked but not mushy, and the consistency sloppy but not soupy.

Add the cooked wild mushrooms, the cheese and butter and stir. Let the risotto rest for a couple of minutes then serve, sprinkled with chopped parsley, shaved truffle and truffle oil. Keep the leftovers to make arancini (see over).

'ARANCINI WITH RAGU & MOZZARELLA'

About 300ml leftover risotto
   (page 92 or 93)
100g meat sauce (page 80 or 82)
100g mozzarella, cut into 10
100g plain flour
1 egg, beaten
100g breadcrumbs
about 500ml vegetable oil

When it comes to leftovers I am a great believer in using up everything. Arancini must have been invented by a very clever Italian cook as they use the leftover meat sauce, any old cheese and leftover risotto. They are great served with a green salad and spicy tomato sauce.

Take a good tablespoonful of cold risotto and press it into the palm of your cupped hand. Put a teaspoon of the meat sauce and a piece of mozzarella in the centre and curl up your hand until you can shape the rice into a ball with the sauce and cheese sealed in the middle. Cover with some more risotto, rolling the lot into a large ball. Repeat with the remaining risotto, sauce and cheese and place the balls in the fridge to set.

Dust the risotto balls in flour, then dip them in the beaten egg and coat with the breadcrumbs. Heat the oil in a deep-fryer or wok and, when the oil starts to shimmer, deep-fry the arancini five at a time. If you are worried they will not be fully cooked you can finish them off in the oven – about 10 minutes at 180°C (gas 4), or until they are hot all the way through.

'PIES STEWS & BRAISES'

My father always said, 'You can't beat a good pie, son!' and no truer word was spoken. Great pies are full of great filling and the great fillings come from rich, slow-cooked beef. The cuts of beef that need this long, gentle cooking process are the tastiest ones by far. A good heavy casserole will be handy for the recipes in this chapter, and cooking them should be carefree. Get used to walking away from the stove while the braise does its bit. The waiting game is rewarded when you lift that lid after hours of cooking and experience the first waft of deliciousness. Don't be tempted to stir a good stew: all you will do is break it up, turning it to mush. But if you do, I suppose you could always make it into a pie!

'POTATO-TOPPED BEEF PIE'

1 sheet ready-rolled shortcrust
   pastry
1 egg, beaten
3 large potatoes, peeled and
   thinly sliced
50g butter, melted, for brushing

filling

50g butter
2 small onions, finely chopped
1kg beef clod without too much
   fat, chopped
250ml beef stock (page 22)
80g plain flour
2 thyme sprigs
2 tbsp Worcestershire sauce
1 handful chopped parsley
salt and pepper
1 pinch grated nutmeg

First make the filling. Melt the butter in saucepan. Add the onions and fry over medium heat until they soften. Add the beef and fry, pressing down with a fork, until it has browned. Drain off the pan juices, adding them to the stock.

Sprinkle the flour over the meat, stir, and continue cooking for another 2 minutes. Remove the pan from the heat and gradually add the stock, mixing well. Return the pan to the heat and stir constantly until the mixture boils and thickens.

Add the thyme, Worcestershire sauce, parsley, salt, pepper and nutmeg. Cover the pan and leave to simmer over a low heat for 30 minutes.

Heat the oven to 240°C (gas 9). Line your pie tin with the shortcrust pastry and prick the base several times with a fork. Cover with a sheet of greaseproof paper and weigh down with baking beans. Bake blind for 20 minutes, then lift out the paper and baking beans and brush the pastry case with beaten egg.

Decrease the oven temperature to 190°C (gas 5). Spoon the filling into the pastry case and top with the sliced potatoes. Brush the potato with lots of melted butter, then put the pie into the oven and bake for 50 minutes to 1 hour. Serve with tomato ketchup.

'COTTAGE PIE'

1 tbsp vegetable oil

2 medium onions, finely chopped

3 large carrots, finely chopped

4 celery sticks, finely chopped

2 leeks, finely chopped

2 garlic cloves, crushed

salt and pepper

1kg mince, but not too fine or fatty

½ bunch thyme

½ bunch rosemary

2 bay leaves

100g plain flour

500ml beef stock

250ml red wine

Worcestershire sauce

brown sauce

1kg mashed potato (page 218-219)

50-100g butter

200ml double cream

2 egg yolks

The great cottage pie... whoever worked this one out was a genius: minced beef, thick gravy, vegetables, and topped with soft mash under a crisp top. The filling needs to be well cooked and the layer of potato should be thick so that it does three jobs: taking up the sauce underneath; staying soft, hot and unctuous in the middle; and being crisp like a chip on top.

Put the oil in a large, heavy pan and start to cook the vegetables and garlic. When they smell like they are frying, add a good amount of salt and pepper and then cook for a few minutes more. Add the mince and fry over a high heat for a good 10 minutes so it has some colour. Taste and adjust the seasoning. Tie the herbs together with string and drop in the pan (you can take out the herbs at the end and you won't have stalks floating in your pie). Sprinkle the flour over the meat and cook for a further 5 minutes (the flour needs to cook a bit or the pie will taste of flour).

Slowly pour in the stock and red wine and simmer for 1 hour until the stock has reduced and the sauce has become thick. Take the pan from the heat and add the Worcestershire and brown sauces to taste, then season with the pepper and salt.

Pour the filling into a big pie dish but only half fill it (you can always make a few little ones and freeze them without the topping for one night when you are all alone).

Heat the oven to 190°C (gas 5). Make your mash as on page 218-219, but please use white pepper when seasoning or it will look like fag ash. While the mash is still hot, beat in some butter and a little cream and then add the eggs – if beaten in well the eggs will make the mash rise as it cooks so that it is light and the top crisp.

Top your mince with the mash, filling the pie dish. Drop some knobs of butter on top and bake for a good 25 minutes – the edges will bubble a bit and the sauce come up the sides, but that's good.

'CORNISH PASTIES'

400g potatoes, peeled and
chopped
200g turnips, peeled and
chopped
100g onions, chopped
salt and pepper
500g chuck or blade braising
steak, finely chopped
1kg ready-rolled puff pastry

There are pasties and there are paaarrstys. In my world, they are still paaarrstys, and to make a great paaarrsty, the vegetables need to be cut into pieces about the same size as a postage stamp but a bit thicker – they don't have to be that even. This recipe makes about eight or ten and you can freeze them raw or cooked. Rest assured, however, that once cooked they will be eaten. So here we go.

Mix together all the vegetables and season with lots of pepper and a little salt. Put them in a colander so the excess water runs off while you do the rest.

Take the finely chopped beef (you can use minced but finely chopped is better) and mix with lots of pepper and a little salt. Break the meat up a little so it is free-flowing rather than one big lump.

Heat the oven to 190°C (gas 5). Cut the pastry into rounds about the size of a 20cm plate. Spoon a good amount of the vegetable mix into the centre of the pastry circles, remembering you are making eight or ten paaarrstys so make sure you have enough for all of them. Sprinkle the meat over (yes, raw).

Dip your finger in some water and rub it around the edge of the pastry circles, then fold each circle up into a half moon shape and seal the two edges together. Gently push the pastry down, then either fold over the edges or simply use a fork to crimp them. Put the pasties on a baking sheet and bake for 45 minutes.

The meat must, must, must be on top of the vegetables otherwise it makes the base of the pasties too soggy.

'AUNTY MARY'S CRUSTED SLOW-COOKED PIE'

2kg stewing steak, such as skirt, shin, brisket, cheek or tail, trimmed of excess fat but leave in all the gristle, then cut into 3cm cubes
80g plain flour
salt and pepper
50ml vegetable oil
2 large onions, roughly chopped
1 litre stock or water
50ml Worcestershire sauce
4 large potatoes, peeled and cut into 3cm chunks

lard pastry

200g lard, at room temperature
400g self-raising flour, sifted
1 pinch salt
180ml cold water
1 egg
a little milk

It's fine to use bought puff pastry here, but lard pastry works really well as it soaks up some of the liquid. The filling is just as good on thick hot buttered toast, so if your pie dish isn't big enough, keep the leftovers.

To make a great pie, the meat has to be cooked long and slow but you want it to be moist and succulent, so only use chunks like shin, skirt, cheek or tail that have plenty of sinew and a little fat so the meat stays together and is moist, not dry and stringy.

Shake the meat and flour in a plastic bag with some salt and pepper – a quick way of coating the meat in the flour with no mess.

Heat a cast-iron or other heavy-based pan over medium heat and add the oil. When hot, fry the onions for about 3 minutes. Add the floured meat and cook until coloured, about 10 minutes. Pour in the stock (or water) and add the Worcestershire sauce. Bring to the boil, reduce the heat to a simmer and cook for about 2 hours.

Add the potatoes and cook gently for a further 1 hour.

Meanwhile, make the pastry. Rub the lard into the flour and salt, or put in a food processor and mix, until resembling breadcrumbs. Add the water bit by bit and mix to a dough. Let rest for 20 minutes.

Check the meat – when ready it will be soft and break apart when squeezed. The sauce should be rich and thick. Season as necessary.

Heat the oven to 190°C (gas 5). Three-quarters fill an ovenproof pie dish with the meat mixture. Roll out the pastry to 3cm thick and cut into a shape large enough to cover the top of the dish. Beat the egg and milk together and brush over the rim of the dish. Press the edges of the pastry down firmly. Brush the pastry with the egg wash, then cut a small hole in the middle to allow steam to escape. Bake for 40 minutes. If the edges of the pastry become too brown, protect with some foil.

Tip The potatoes are added for flavour and texture and to bulk out the meat, therefore making the dish more cost effective, but most importantly they help thicken the sauce.

'PARTY PIES'

pastry case
450g plain flour

1 tsp salt

105g beef dripping

pastry lids
500g ready-rolled puff pastry

1 egg, beaten

filling
50g butter, plus extra for
   greasing

salt and pepper

1kg onions, minced

1kg minced beef

100g plain flour

1 pinch nutmeg

2 tsp soy sauce

500ml beef stock (page 22)

As an Aussie I have been privileged to grow up with the meat pie. Not just the grand mince beef pie that is the stalwart of every Aussie rules game, but the party pie – small enough to hold and just two bites. On serving, the lid is lifted and tomato ketchup poured in before the lid is replaced (this ritual is paramount to the enjoyment of the pie). You can use this recipe to make one or several larger pies instead of tiny ones.

Make the pastry for the cases the night before: sift the flour and salt into a basin. Put the dripping in a saucepan with 300ml water and heat, stirring, until the dripping melts. Remove from the heat. Make a well in the centre of the dry ingredients and pour in the liquid, stirring to make a dough. Wrap the pastry in cling film and leave it to rest in the fridge overnight.

To make the filling, melt the butter in a large frying pan and season with lots of pepper and some salt. Add the onions and cook, stirring, for 5 minutes until the onions are soft but not brown. Add the mince and cook, stirring, for 5 minutes. Sprinkle over the flour, stir, and keep cooking to get rid of the raw taste of the flour. Add the nutmeg, then the soy sauce and stock and bring to the boil. Simmer for 10 minutes until cooked through. Set aside to cool.

When ready to put the pies together, heat the oven to 240°C (gas 9) and grease the pie tins or dishes.

Roll out the pastry for the bases and cut out circles slightly larger than your pie tins. Line the pie tins with the pastry, then fill with the cold meat filling. Take the puff pastry and cut out lids for the pies. Dampen the rims of the pastry cases with water and press the pastry lids on to seal. Brush the tops lightly with beaten egg.

Place the pies in the oven. Reduce the temperature to 190°C (gas 5) and cook for 20-25 minutes, until the tops are very brown.

'PIE FLOATERS WITH PEA SOUP'

4-6 meat pies (page 105)
tomato ketchup

soup
30g butter
1 shallot, diced
salt and pepper
200g dried peas, soaked
200ml beef stock (page 22)
150g fresh peas

Take a good Aussie meat pie and serve it in a bowl of pea soup – yes really. But to make it work it needs a glug of dead horse, as my father used to call it – that would be tomato sauce or ketchup to you and me. He had a great little poem (if you could call it that) he'd recite when topping his pie: 'Shake and shake and shake the bottle, none will come and then a lot'll!'

Make the pies following the recipe on the previous page, but cut the pastry larger to fit pie tins that are 12-15cm in diameter. Bake them for 20-25 minutes.

To make the soup, in a decent-sized saucepan, melt the butter and add the diced shallot. Season and cook for 3 minutes, until the shallot is transparent but without colour. Add the dried peas and a good amount of salt and black pepper. Cover with the stock, bring to the boil and cook for 20 minutes.

Add the fresh peas, bring the pan back to the boil and cook for 5 minutes. Purée the soup somehow (there are so many ways to do it these days, it's incredible). Taste and season as necessary.

Divide the soup among serving bowls and top with the cooked meat pies. Serve with tomato ketchup.

'BOEUF À LA FICELLE'

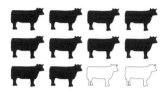

1.5kg piece beef rump

4 leeks, white parts only

1 large onion, stuck with 1 clove

2 large carrots, peeled and
  chopped

2 large turnips, peeled and
  chopped

1 bouquet garni

salt and pepper

An absolute classic French dish. For this, the beef has to be top-quality and cut from the rump.

You will need some kitchen string. Tie up the piece of beef, leaving a long section of string attached. Bundle the leeks together and tie them up too. Put all the vegetables and the bouquet garni in a pot with 3.4 litres salted water, bring them to a simmer and cook for 1 hour.

Drop the meat into the pot, leaving the end of the string hanging outside. Boil first for 5 minutes, then reduce the heat and allow to cook gently for 30 minutes.

Use the string to pull the meat from the pot. You will find it tender, rather underdone and imbued with the flavour of the vegetables and herbs. If it is too rare for your taste, return it to the pot for a few minutes more.

Discard the bouquet garni. Lift out the onion and cut it into quarters. Arrange the meat on a large hot serving dish and garnish with the vegetables. Serve with other vegetables, such as small steamed potatoes and french beans, either cooked separately or with the beef if you prefer.

'BEEF STROGANOFF'

500g beef fillet
60ml vegetable or corn oil
salt and black pepper
12 button mushrooms, sliced
60ml brandy
100ml double cream

spätzle
100g plain flour
1 egg
1 tbsp warm milk
salt
melted butter

Properly cooked, beef stroganoff is a beautiful dish and great with spätzle or mash, or even mash and a fried egg. The pepper, when cooked with the beef, is just teeth-grindingly delicious.

To make the spätzle, mix the flour, egg, milk and a little salt together to make a dough. Push the dough through a spätzle tray if you have one, otherwise fit a piping bag with a small nozzle, fill it with the dough and squeeze it out into matchstick lengths, like little short worms.

Bring a big pot of water to the boil and drop in the noodles – they take about 2 minutes to cook. Drain well then drop them into some melted butter, season and keep warm.

To make the stroganoff, cut the beef into thin strips the size of your little finger and put them in a big bowl. Meanwhile, heat the biggest and heaviest frying pan you've got – get it seriously hot. Add the oil to the beef, season it really well with lots of pepper and some salt, and mix together.

Drop the beef into the hot pan and do not touch it for 1 minute – let it sizzle. Sniff the air and smell the way the pepper roasts while the beef is cooking. Only once the beef starts to brown can you stir it. Cook for another minute. Keep that heat high, stir in the mushrooms and cook again for a minute. By now the meat should have colour but not be dry.

Add the brandy – it should sizzle. Strike a match and burn off some of the booze, but not all of it as you need a punch. The alcohol will help make a great sauce by picking up all the flavours stuck on the base of the pan.

Shake the pan and then add the cream. Shake again and bring to the boil – it should boil fast – then serve with the spätzle.

'BEEF STEW & DUMPLINGS'

2kg stewing steak such as beef shin or neck, diced
100g plain flour
salt and pepper
30g beef dripping or lard, melted
225g onions, sliced
675g potatoes, quartered
1 litre beef stock (page 22)

dumplings
300g suet
700g self-raising flour
300ml warm water

Now you cannot go wrong here. This simple but very delicious stew really is a leave-it-to-cook wonder. Everything gets put in one pot then goes into the oven. I like to seal the meat well as I think it helps the taste. Use a cut with real flavour like shin or neck, but let it cook slow and long and it will be delicious.

Heat the oven to 190°C (gas 5) and trim any excess fat from the diced meat. Take a large plastic bag, put the flour in it and season well. Drop the meat in the bag and shake it like mad to coat all the meat in the flour.

Melt the dripping or lard in a casserole. Add the meat and onions and fry well, stirring all the time. Add the potatoes and stir. Pour in the stock (or even water) and stir, scraping the bottom of the pan to take up the flour and all that flavour.

Cover with a lid (or foil). Put the stew in the oven, reduce the heat to 140°C (gas 1) and shut the door and cook for 3 hours... then it will be ready.

To make the dumplings, mix the suet, flour and some salt in a big bowl and stir in the warm water – this will make a heavy mixture. Roll the dumplings into balls about the size of golf balls.

Take about 100ml of gravy from the stew and put it in a saucepan with 500ml water. Bring to the boil. You will need to cook the dumplings in batches so drop half of them in the pan and cook for 10 minutes, turning so they cook evenly and puff up – YUM.

Lift the dumplings out of the broth and keep warm while you cook the remainder. You can either serve them in a bowl separately from the stew, or gently stir them into the stew before serving, which I think is better.

'BRAISED BEEF WITH STAR ANISE'

6 star anise

1 handful cassia bark

2 lemongrass stalks

vegetable oil

1 beef shin, boned

500ml beef stock (page 22)

1 handful sliced galangal

2 red chillies, deseeded and
   sliced

6 lime leaves, torn

30ml fish sauce

100ml light soy sauce

200g rock sugar

This works really well both hot as a stew with noodles and sliced and served cold in a salad.

Rinse the star anise and cassia bark thoroughly in a sieve, then roast in a wok or dry frying pan until dark (but not too dark) and fragrant. Tip them on to a piece of muslin and tie into a bundle so they are easy to remove from the pan during cooking. Cut the lemongrass into pieces 6cm long and leave them unpeeled.

Take a pot and heat a little bit of oil in it. Brown the shin over a high heat until it is dark in colour. Once dark, remove the meat and clean the pot.

Pour the stock into the pot and add the spice bag, galangal, lemongrass, chillies, lime leaves, fish sauce, soy sauce and sugar. Bring to the boil then add the meat and simmer slowly for 2½ hours. Alternatively you can cook it, uncovered, in a 180°C (gas 4) oven for the same amount of time, adding more liquid if need be and turning the meat regularly.

Take the meat from the pot. Strain the sauce and return the meat to it. If you are going to serve the meat with noodles, shred it; or you can chill the meat and then slice it very thinly to serve in a salad with a little of the sauce and some shredded raw vegetables.

'BEEF RENDANG WITH LEMONGRASS & GINGER'

2 lemongrass stalks

40g coriander seeds

1 tsp cumin seeds

1 tsp turmeric powder

100g block coconut cream

3 large onions, finely chopped

6 garlic cloves, chopped

6 red chillies, deseeded and
   chopped

2 thumb-sized pieces ginger,
   peeled and chopped

2 bay leaves

1.5kg stewing beef, cut into
   2.5cm cubes

2 x 400g cans coconut milk

500ml strong veal or beef stock,
   heated

sticky rice, to serve

This is a Muslim dish from Sumatra in Indonesia. By the time the big pot of liquid has cooked down to a kind of beef in jam, the meat is so tender and melting it reminds me of the best meat pies. Shin is, for me, the very best cut to use here. The pan you use needs to be wide rather than deep so that the liquid boils off as the beef cooks.

Pound the lemongrass to a pulp using a mortar and pestle. Gently toast the coriander and cumin seeds and the turmeric in a dry frying pan until fragrant, then grind to a powder, or pound with the pestle until the spices are as smooth as possible.

In a wide pan (I use a cast-iron wok), heat the block of coconut cream until it melts but keep the heat low so it does not burn. Drop in the onions, garlic, chillies, ginger and pounded lemongrass and cook gently until the onions have softened and the mixture starts to smell beautiful and fragrant. Add the ground spices and the bay leaves and fry for a few minutes more until the mixture is really bursting with aroma.

Add the meat, increase the heat under the pan so it browns it well, and stir until it is completely coated with the spices – this will take a few minutes. Add the coconut milk, bring to the boil, then add the hot stock. Turn the heat up to high and continue cooking – the level of the liquid will quickly fall. Please stir occasionally until the sauce reduces to a thick paste, then keep cooking and stirring until the sauce becomes thick like lava and really coats the meat (this will take a good hour). Serve the rendang with sticky rice.

'BRAISED OXTAIL & CELERIAC MASH'

2 oxtails, trimmed of excess fat
and cut into chunks

salt and pepper

50g plain flour

4 carrots

2 leeks

6 celery stalks

2 bunches flat-leaf parsley

2 small sage branches

about 6 tbsp olive oil

400g piece bacon, cut into large
chunks

200g veal shin, or 1 pig's trotter

750ml red wine

celeriac mash

1 large celeriac, peeled and
diced

2 large potatoes, peeled and
diced

100ml milk

100ml olive oil

salt and pepper

Here long, slow cooking produces juicy, sinewy, sticky meat that just has to be eaten with your fingers. My restaurant version of celeriac mash may seem a little over the top but this root veg deserves great treatment. Beware of serving it liberally as it is very rich indeed. If you want to spice it up a little, add a chunk of fresh horseradish. The recipe also works with parsnips.

Heat the oven to 190°C (gas 5). Season the oxtail well and dust with flour. Tie the carrots, leek, celery and herbs tightly in a bundle.

Heat the oil in a cast-iron casserole or big, heavy ovenproof pan. Add the bacon, cook for 2 minutes, then add the oxtail and leave to sit and sizzle. Wait until well browned, then they will easily come away from the pan. Turn them over and cook for a further 3 minutes, making sure to move the bacon too so it doesn't burn.

When the meat is browned all over, add the bundle of vegetables and the shin or trotter. Add the wine and bring to the boil to drive off the raw alcohol. Let it bubble away for about 10 minutes or so, while you scrape the sticky bits of meat from the bottom of the pot.

Pour in 2 litres water or enough almost to cover the meat. Carefully press a double sheet of baking paper into the liquid to moisten it. Cover with the lid. Cook in the oven for 3½ hours, until the liquid has reduced right down and the meat is falling apart. Change the paper during cooking if it becomes too skanky and crisp.

To make the mash, put the vegetables in a heavy-based saucepan. Add the milk, olive oil, salt and pepper, then enough water to make sure all the vegetables are covered. Place over a medium heat, bring to the boil and cook for about 15-20 minutes until the vegetables are all soft. Drain off and reserve the cooking liquid. Mash the veg with a fork, then mix in the reserved liquid, making the mash as sloppy as you like – the sloppier the better for me.

'DAUBE À LA JDT'

2kg brisket
salt and pepper
olive oil
2 carrots, chopped
1 onion, chopped
1 celery stalk, chopped
1 garlic clove, crushed
2 whole star anise
100ml port
400ml red wine
1 pig's trotter
300ml beef stock (page 22)
4 tbsp dark soy sauce
1 x 440ml can Guinness
2 tbsp fish sauce
mashed potatoes (page 218-219),
    to serve

Brisket is the classic cut for the salt beef sandwich – it is also the true pastrami cut, thin and flat but taken from the rib. The French make braises from brisket on the bone and stew it for long periods with pigs' feet to give a thick and sticky, gelatinous sauce.

The recipe below is for brisket off the bone and it should be served sparingly with mashed potato. Some would call it a daube, I say it is bloody good braised brisket with red wine. Oxtail works a treat in this recipe too, but takes a little longer.

Heat the oven to 190°C (gas 5). Trim most of the excess fat from the brisket, leaving some for colour and flavour. Cut the meat into big hunks, about 6cm squares, and season really well. Heat a little olive oil in a frying pan, add the brisket and fry until well browned on all sides.

Heat some more oil in a casserole. Add the vegetables and star anise and cook briefly, until the vegetables are just soft. Pour in the port and red wine, and allow to bubble until the liquid has reduced by half.

Add the brisket and pig's trotter to the casserole and cover with the stock. Bring to the boil, skim any scum from the surface, then add the soy sauce, Guinness and fish sauce. Transfer to the oven and cook for 2 hours, or until the meat is very tender.

Take the casserole from the oven, lift out the meat and keep it warm. Strain the sauce and return the liquid to the casserole dish with the pig's trotter. Bring to the boil and keep bubbling until the sauce is thick. Taste and adjust the seasoning as necessary.

Lift the pig's trotter from the sauce and keep the meat from it to serve on toast – yum! Drop the beef back into the sauce and return to the oven for a final 30 minutes. Serve with mashed potatoes.

'BOLLITO MISTO'

4 carrots
4 onions
4 celery stalks
1 pig's trotter
3 sage branches
4 black peppercorns
1kg veal shank, bone in
1kg salt beef
1 large chicken
sea salt
1 cotechino, or similar sausage
1 zampone
1kg cooked, pickled ox tongue

to serve
John's green sauce (page 120)
mustard fruits

The idea of a modern bollito misto is to keep the meat boiling gently for not too long, without stirring things around, so that all the meats and the vegetables stay whole and you hit a balance of great stock and lovely tender meat that retains all its flavour. The classic way to serve bollito misto is with bowls of salsa verde (green sauce) and mustard fruits (fruits preserved in a mustard-flavoured syrup). You can buy jars of mustard fruits from any good Italian deli (the best is known as Mostarda di Cremona). The deli is also where you will find the cotechino (an Italian pork salame) and zampone (sausage encased in a pig's trotter).

Put the whole vegetables and pig's trotter in the largest pot you can find. Cover with cold water, then add the sage and the peppercorns. Bring to the boil, to 'wash' the trotter, then discard the water.

Add the veal shank and salt beef and start again with fresh water to cover. (The idea is to end up with really clear, pure stock.) Cook at a slow simmer for about 2 hours, skimming at regular intervals.

Add the chicken and more cold water to cover. Bring up to the boil again, skim the surface as before, then turn the heat back down to a slow simmer. Cook for another 1½ hours or so, until all the meat is cooked. Taste the liquid and add salt if necessary.

Add the cotechino, zampone and tongue. Top up with cold water again, bring to the boil and skim. Turn the heat to a slow simmer and cook for another 30 minutes, until the sausages and tongue are heated through and the broth is lovely and rich and clear.

Remove the meats and put on platters. Take out the vegetables and cut them into small pieces, then put them on a serving dish. Put them all in the middle of the table with bowls of green sauce and mustard fruits. Cut the meats into chunky pieces and let people help themselves to everything.

'STEAK & KIDNEY PUDDING'

2kg beef shin, off the bone

salt and pepper

2 carrots

1 leek

3 celery stalks

1 bunch flat-leaf parsley

1 small sage branch

3 tbsp olive oil

about 200g piece of bacon, cut in chunks

1 veal shin or pig's trotter

about 375ml red wine

4 lambs' kidneys

suet dough

350g plain flour

125g butter, plus extra for greasing

125g suet

1 tsp salt

½ tsp sugar

1-2 tbsp warm water

You can use beef or lamb kidneys for this recipe. In the restaurant we would braise oxtail in veal stock to make a rich, gelatinous filling. Shin of beef is used here, with some veal shin or pig's trotter, which will also make the sauce thick and unctuous. The trotter you can discard after cooking, or take the bone out, roll the meat up in cling film and leave it in the fridge for a while to firm it up, then fry it for supper.

Heat the oven to 190°C (gas 5). Cut the beef into hunks about the size of your hand and season it generously – remember this is the base of the sauce and the filling so it needs to be seasoned really well. Tie the carrots, leek, celery and herbs tightly in a bundle.

Heat the oil in a large heavy pan – enamelled cast-iron is good. Add the bacon and beef and let them sit and sizzle. Don't shake the pan or try to flip the beef too early, although you can move the bacon around. Wait until the beef is well browned underneath – the pieces will lift off when ready. Once you've browned both sides, add the vegetable bundle and the veal shin or trotter. Pour in the wine and bring to the boil to drive off the raw alcohol, then let it reduce for about 10 minutes, scraping the sticky bits from the bottom.

Pour in about 2 litres water, so that it almost covers the meat. Add the kidneys and stir well. Cover with baking paper and carefully press this into the liquid to moisten it so that it doesn't burn. Transfer the pan to the oven for about 2½ hours, until the liquid has reduced right down and the meat is virtually falling apart. Change the paper once during cooking, as it will absorb all the fat and impurities, leaving a lovely clear, shiny sauce.

Remove from the oven and let cool a little. Take out the kidneys, chop into thumb-sized pieces and set aside in a bowl. Take out the vegetables, chop roughly and mix with the kidneys. Take the meat out and chop it, but keep it chunky. Remove the shin or trotter.

Place the pan back on the stove, bring the sauce to the boil and reduce to the consistency of good gravy. Taste and season. Leave to cool (added to the pudding hot the dough will collapse).

To make the suet dough, combine all the ingredients in a bowl. Knead lightly to give a smooth dough but try not to overwork or the heat of your hands will melt the suet and the crust will be heavy. Roll out one-third of the dough into a round large enough to cover the top of a 1.7 litre pudding basin and set aside. Grease the inside of the basin with a little butter. Cut a round of greaseproof paper to fit the bottom of the basin, moisten it with water to make it pliable and press inside. Roll out the larger piece of dough into a circle big enough to line the basin, leaving a small overhang around the top, then press it gently into the basin. Add the kidney and vegetable mixture to the basin, then the meat, then fill with the gravy. Keep the remaining gravy to serve with the pudding. Put the pastry lid on, bring the overhang over the top, moisten the underside with water and press gently to seal. Cover the top with a double sheet of moistened greaseproof paper, tie with string and wrap the whole thing in foil.

Take a large lidded pan and place a folded tea towel in the bottom to keep the basin away from direct heat. Sit the basin in the pan and add enough boiling water to come three-quarters of the way up the side. Put the lid on and leave to simmer for about 4½ hours, topping up the water level when necessary.

When the pudding is cooked, unwrap it and turn it out onto a serving plate. Pour some gravy over.... lucky you!

STEAKS & BIG HUNKS

The mighty bovine is a versatile beast. Laying on his back is Britain's most prized hunk – the rump, loin and rib and, sitting inside the rib, the fillet. Collectively this area is called the pistol. It is the least used or worked part of the beast, so the meat is tender, with fat that lays in the muscle and melts as it cooks – that's why it can be cut into steaks and cooked quickly, or left in big hunks and slowly roasted. Many people make fun of the British fascination for roast beef, but let me tell you: done well there are few things better. A hunk of rib roasted in a hot oven will deliver flavour, texture and aroma, and feed a whole family, like few things in this world. In this chapter you will also learn to cook steak, but do me a favour: relax and enjoy cooking it! If you feel you are not in control your steak will misbehave. Remember you are the master.

'HOW TO COOK A GREAT STEAK'

Cooking steak is a joy because it is a terrific piece of meat with great flavour whether grilled or fried, and really there are no rules. Apart from this: eat the steak cooked the way you like it and tell steak snobs to rack off – we all have personal taste.

I suggest frying the more delicate cuts such as fillet and maybe young sirloin, and grilling the bigger, tastier, fattier ones like the rump, rib or anything on a bone, such as côte de boeuf or T-bone.

It is hard to say how long to cook a steak because each one varies in thickness and structure. But generally, for medium steak, I'd sear for 2 minutes on each side, then cook a minute extra for each centimetre of thickness – so a 2cm-thick sirloin served medium will take about 6 minutes total. If there is a bone, it will be more like 2 minutes extra per centimetre.

Pan-frying

Use a solid pan that will hold the heat well, nothing flimsy. A black cast-iron pan is perfect. Always heat the pan for a long time, and if your steak is really thick, heat the oven to 200°C (gas 6) a good 15 minutes before you start to cook it. Rub the steak with ample oil – vegetable oil, nothing stronger as the steak tastes great itself. Season with salt and pepper after it is covered with oil or the salt will start to eat into the meat and dry it out.

Open a window and a door to get fresh air because you are going to have lots of smoke. Drop the steak into the pan when it is so hot it is hard to put your hand close to it. Don't touch the steak for 2 minutes. Then turn it over and, if it is not sizzling, add some more oil but keep that heat high. Sear for 2 minutes more and then turn again (unless you like your steak blue).

If it is really thick, say 5-7.5cm, put the pan in the oven (no need to double the washing up) for around 4 minutes, depending on how you want it cooked. You won't ever need to leave it in for more than 8 minutes; if you do it will be cremated.

Take the steak out and leave it to rest for 5 minutes before you serve. Remember the steak will continue to cook while it is resting. Drop a huge blob of butter in the pan before you set it aside – the butter in the bottom, oh that's good.

Griddle

Put a ridged cast-iron plate over a high heat for 10 minutes before you even think about cooking. Rub the steak with oil and season it with salt and pepper on both sides. Open the window so the smoke can escape.

Lay the steak on the griddle and leave it for 2 minutes, then flip and do the same. Cook as long as you need, then take the steak off and leave it to rest.

As with the pan-fried steak, if the meat is really thick, put it in the oven while it is still on the griddle plate.

Grilling over coals

To cook steaks over coals, follow the same principles as when using a griddle plate but keep an eye out for yellow flames. This means the fat has caught fire – you don't want the taste of burnt fat on your meat, so move the steak to another part of the grill.

Creamed Horseradish

You could buy horseradish cream and I would not scream at you but if you do get the chance to buy some fresh horseradish and make your own you will really be able to tell the difference. Buy a whole horseradish and wrap it in cling film and it will keep for a few weeks in the fridge, or grate the whole thing and mix it with 100ml white wine vinegar and a pinch of salt – stored in a sealed jar, it lasts for weeks.

2 tbsp grated horseradish in vinegar
100ml soured cream
1 pinch salt

Squeeze out any excess vinegar from the grated horseradish. Lightly whip the cream and salt. Mix the whole lot together and boom.

Just Mustard

If there ever was a marriage made in heaven, it has to be steak and mustard. Whoever it was that first made mustard was a very clever person indeed. There are a number of varieties available: English, which is the hottest; dijon or French mustard, which has a kick but is a little milder; American, which is sweet; and plenty more. I'd go for English mustard with a really full-bodied steak like a rump, or a well-aged sirloin, and French for a fillet. The American mustard I leave for the hotdogs – beef ones, I mean. Quality kosher beef hotdogs are delicious!

Hollandaise Sauce

6 tbsp white wine
6 tbsp white wine vinegar
20 black peppercorns
2 bay leaves
3 egg yolks
300g warm melted butter
1 pinch salt
juice of ½ lemon

Boil the first 4 ingredients in a pan for 5-8 minutes, until reduced to about 3 tablespoons. Let cool, then strain. Put the egg yolks in a large stainless steel bowl and set over a pan of barely simmering water. Whisk in a tablespoon of the vinegar reduction. Continue whisking until it turns pale and the whisk leaves a pattern in the sauce. Remove the bowl from the heat and gradually whisk in the butter. Add a tablespoon of water if you feel the sauce might be about to scramble. Beat in the salt and lemon juice. Serves 4.

Grilled Mushrooms

Whether it be for breakfast with a poached egg, or to serve alongside steak, this is the best way I know to grill a whole big grown-up flat mushroom. Remember they are meaty in their own right so should you have a friend who's (oh god, am I going to say this...?) A VEGETARIAN (ahhhhhh!) you can always just serve them these instead.

12 large flat field mushrooms
50ml olive oil
salt and pepper

Put the mushrooms on a baking tray, stems facing upwards. Drizzle generously with olive oil. Sprinkle with salt and freshly ground black pepper and grill slowly, at a fair distance from the heat, until cooked. The mushrooms should be very dark in colour but still very moist. Leave to cool a bit before serving.

Onion Rings

700ml vegetable oil, for deep-frying
60ml soda water, chilled
120g cornflour, plus 20g for dusting
1 large pinch salt
2 ice cubes
1 large white or brown onion, skinned and second
    layer removed

Heat the oil gently in a deep-fryer over a medium heat. The oil will start to shimmer when ready. Whisk the soda water, cornflour and salt to a paste. Add ice cubes and keep cool.

Put a kettle of water on to boil. Slice the onion into rounds about 1cm thick and place in a large heatproof bowl. Pour the boiling water over the rings and stir well. Drain and pat dry. Dust all the rings with the extra cornflour and dip in the batter.

Drop the onion rings in the oil one at a time (you want about ten per batch). Raise the heat if necessary to keep them frying. When the onion rings float to the surface, keep cooking for another minute, then drain on kitchen paper. Serves 4.

Béarnaise Sauce

100ml white wine vinegar
1 shallot, chopped
a few sprigs of tarragon
2 egg yolks
120g warm melted butter
salt and pepper

Put the vinegar, shallot and tarragon in a saucepan and boil until the mixture has reduced by about three-quarters. Allow to cool and pour into in a large stainless steel bowl.

Set the bowl over a pan of barely simmering water. Add the egg yolks and whisk until you can see the whisk leaving a pattern in the sauce.

Remove the bowl from the heat and start to add the melted butter, little by little, whisking all the time until all the butter is used or your arm has fallen off! Sitting the bowl on a folded cloth will help to keep the heat in. Season with good salt and plenty of pepper. Serves 2.

Mustard Sauce

This has to be one of the simplest but best mustard sauce recipes ever. I learnt it at Le Pont de la Tour and I have used it for everything, from beef to veal to kidneys and even roast pigeon. This recipe makes enough for four steaks with some left over to be served cold on things like cold roast beef.

300ml single cream
300ml dijon mustard
1 handful chopped parsley

Put the cream in a heavy-based saucepan, bring it to the boil, then let it boil for a few minutes. What we want is for the cream to reduce by half, at which point we use a whisk to beat in the mustard. Take it from the heat, throw in the parsley, give it a stir, and that's it.

Ceps Bordelaise Sauce

2 tbsp vegetable oil
50g butter
2 large shallots, finely chopped
1 garlic clove, crushed to paste
400g fresh ceps
200ml good red wine
1 thumb-sized piece bone marrow (optional)
2 handfuls chopped parsley

Heat a large pan and add the oil and the butter. Cook the shallots gently for a few minutes, stirring until soft – don't let them brown. Add the garlic and continue to cook, stirring often. Slice the ceps the width of your little finger, drop them in with the shallots and stir, shake and cook for 5 minutes until it all smells delicious. Add the wine, and the bone marrow (if using). Boil for 3 minutes, then take it off the heat and add the parsley.

For a richer sauce you can add more wild mushrooms and finish with a few drops of cream.

'CÔTE DE BOEUF WITH CARAMELIZED SHALLOTS'

2 large ribs of beef, about
   700g each
pepper

caramelized shallots
50ml vegetable oil
12 whole banana shallots
50g butter
2 bay leaves
1 thyme sprig
sea salt
250ml beef or veal stock
   (see page 22 or 24)

This huge hunk of meat takes time. In butchers' terms there are five ribs to be cut into Côte de Boeuf, each one with the meat hanging freely but with plenty of fat. I often cook this with all the fat so I get all the flavour, then trim off some of the fat before I carve it. Because this is a big, well-used muscle, I do not believe that it should be too rare or it will be tough; the sinew and the fat need to break down.

Heat the oil in a frying pan, add the shallots and colour them over a high heat. Once coloured, drain off and throw away the oil. Add the butter, bay, thyme and some salt to the pan. Cook for a good 5 minutes, turning and shaking the shallots, but try not to burn the butter.

Add enough stock just to cover the base of the pan and allow the liquid to bubble away before adding any more; the sauce will reduce and become sticky while cooking the shallots at the same time. Continue until the shallots are very soft and have a thick buttery and beefy glaze.

Meanwhile, heat a griddle plate and season the beef well, remembering that it is thick. Score the fat a little and lay the cutlet fat-side down on the griddle. That fat will start to melt and this is what is going to flavour the outside of this great big beauty.

Once the fat starts to char, let it fall naturally on to one side and leave the beef to cook for 4 minutes. Turn it over and cook for another 4 minutes. Turn again, but do it so that you rotate the meat by 180 degrees and grill for 2 more minutes. Flip it over, then put in a hot oven for about 6 minutes for a medium steak. Let it rest for 5 minutes before serving it whole.....you have to show off!!!

'THE BIG CHIP'

6 large potatoes
corn or vegetable oil, for
   deep-frying
salt

Peel the potatoes and cut them into chips 3cm thick. Soak them in cool water for 5 minutes, then change the water and leave for 5 more minutes. Place on a towel or paper and pat dry.

Meanwhile, heat the oil in your deep-fryer. My rule is 5 litres oil to 500g potatoes, so you may have to cook in batches.

Blanching is the middle process used by all chippies and restaurants around the country who like the chips well-cooked and fluffy on the inside but crisp on the outside. To do it, heat the oil to 140°C. Place the chips in the oil and cook for 8-10 minutes. Lift them from the oil and drain well, then place them on a tray to cool.

The next stage of the cooking is the frying. This process should be quick and the oil must be hot. The quantity of chips added to the oil will determine how quickly the oil is able to return to the temperature required to seal and brown the outside of the chip and make the inside all fluffy.

Heat the oil to 190°C and lower the basket of chips into the oil. Leave to cook for 2 minutes, then give them a little shake and cook for a further 4-5 minutes until they are well-coloured and crisp. Take the chips from the oil and drain thoroughly for a few minutes before putting them in a bowl and sprinkling with salt.

'RUMP STEAK SANDWICHES WITH ROCKET & PARMESAN'

6 rump steaks, 150g each

2 tbsp vegetable oil

salt and pepper

100g parmesan cheese

1 small loaf of unsliced bread,
    multigrain or white and crusty

butter, for spreading

100g rocket

This has been a staple dish of the ground floor at Smiths since the day we opened. It is a perfect combination – juicy steak with peppery rocket and strong parmesan. The bread will soak up any excess juice for you to enjoy. I really like these sandwiches and, after you have tried one, they will become a favourite for barbecues and picnics alike. With the advent of portable and disposable barbecues, you could easily cook these little beauties out in the open, whilst flying a kite.

Using a rolling pin or meat mallet, bash the steaks so they are about 2-3cm thick.

Heat a griddle pan over a high heat (or prepare a barbecue). Rub the steaks well with oil and place on the hot griddle. Season and cook for 2 minutes on the first side, then turn and cook until the steaks are done to your liking – I cook mine for only 4 minutes, as I like a rare-ish steak.

Meanwhile, shave the parmesan using a veggie peeler, as if you were peeling a carrot.

Cut 12 slices from the bread and butter well. Lay six pieces out on a bench, butter-side up. Sprinkle a little parmesan over and put the cooked steak on top. Use the remaining parmesan to cover the steak, then pile on the rocket. Place the other pieces of bread on top. For the sandwiches to really work and hold together you need to press down on them. Finally, cut them in half and wrap in greaseproof paper – they should last a few hours that way.

'PEPPER STEAK'

50g black peppercorns
4 fillet steaks, each about 250g
75g butter
3 tbsp beef stock (page 22)
4 tbsp brandy
1 tbsp double cream (optional)

This is one steak dish that is best done with fillet, because you need that thickness to give the right ratio of meat to pepper, otherwise it will be uncomfortably hot. I like this steak served with just the buttery, peppery juices, but some people like to add a touch of cream at the end. It's up to you.

Crush the peppercorns in a food processor or with a mortar and pestle, then sieve them to remove all the dust, which will otherwise catch in your throat. Press the remainder into both sides of the steaks.

Heat 50g of the butter in a heavy frying pan over a medium heat. Add the steaks and leave them alone until you can see they are forming a golden crust underneath. Turn them over and cook until medium-rare – roughly 3 minutes on each side, or more if you prefer.

Remove the steaks from the pan and keep them warm. Raise the heat under the pan, add the stock and the brandy and flame it carefully to burn off the alcohol. Whisk in the rest of the butter, scraping the bottom of the pan to incorporate all the tasty scraps. If using cream, add it to the sauce now. Either way, bring the sauce briefly to the boil and pour it over the steak to serve.

ALSO GOOD WITH STEAK: Big hunks of roast parsnip and carrot 🐄 Sticky 🐄 Ratatouille 🐄 New potatoes, rosemary and loads of black pepper

'BREAKFAST STEAK WITH EGGS, MUSHROOMS & TOAST'

400g large flat mushrooms
100ml vegetable oil
salt and pepper
2 shallots, diced
2 garlic cloves, chopped
2 handfuls flat-leaf parsley, chopped
4 thick slices sourdough bread
4 sirloin steaks, about 175g each
1 lemon

As breakfast goes, mushrooms on toast – in particular very thick, hot, well-buttered toast – is good. Add a few eggs, some seasoning and a few herbs and that breakfast becomes a feast. Add a good piece of steak and it becomes an all-day fantasy. For this you need really large flat mushrooms as big as saucers.

Heat the grill. Sit the mushrooms open-side up on a baking tray, drizzle with 50ml oil and season with salt and pepper. Grill for 8-10 minutes, then remove and leave to cool slightly.

Put another 50ml oil in a large frying pan. Add the shallots and cook for 2 minutes, then add the garlic and cook for a further 2 minutes. Remove from the pan and set aside.

Slice the mushrooms thickly. Add them to the pan and leave them to cook for 4 minutes or so, without moving, until the underside starts to brown. Turn and cook for 2 minutes more. Season and add the cooked shallots and garlic, together with the parsley.

Arrange the mushrooms into four circles, each with a hole in the centre. Crack an egg into each hole (add more oil if the pan is getting too dry). Cook until the white is firm but the yolk still soft.

Meanwhile, set a ridged cast-iron plate over a high heat for 10 minutes. Rub the steak with oil and season on both sides. Open the window so the smoke can escape. Place the steak on the griddle and leave for 2 minutes, then flip and do the same. Cook as long as you need and then set the steaks aside to rest.

Toast the slices of bread. Squeeze some lemon juice over the steak. Breakfast is up guys!

fried onions and fried egg ☛ Aubergines and black bean sauce ☛ Tomato, mozzarella and basil salad ☛ Creamy mash and mustard

'CARPET BAG STEAK'

4 fillet steaks, about 175g each
8 oysters in the shell
4 large strips streaky bacon
vegetable oil
salt and pepper
200g butter

This is an Australian classic – steak stuffed with fresh oysters, then wrapped in strips of streaky bacon and fried. It is important not to drain the oysters of too much of their liquid (you need to reserve this for later) as its saltiness tenderizes and flavours the meat and keeps the oysters lovely and moist. When the steak is cooked to your liking, take it out of the pan, remove the pan from the heat and add the drained oyster juice, then scrape up the bits from the bottom of the pan and pour the resulting liquid over the steak.

Take each fillet and slice a sharp knife into the side to make a pocket – not all the way through or that won't be a pocket.

Shuck (that is, open) the oysters and release them from their shells, draining off and keeping the juice. Put four oysters back in their shells to serve on the side of the steaks. Take the other oysters and put one inside the pocket of each steak. Pour in some of the juice – this salty water acts as a seasoning and keeps the oyster and the beef moist. We love things moist!

Wrap each fillet with the bacon and stick a toothpick in to hold it all together. Put a solid, heavy-based pan on the heat and get it super-hot. Open the window as there is about to be a good amount of smoke. Rub the steaks all over with oil and season with salt and a little pepper.

Put the steaks in the pan and cook for a good 3 minutes each side, then turn the heat down and cook for 2 more minutes each side. Add the butter and any leftover oyster juice. If you want to cook the fillets well done then they need to go into a not-too-hot oven for about 5 minutes to finish.

Serve your steaks with chips (page 134) or a big tomato salad... come on, you know how to make a tomato salad.

'SURF & TURF'

6 fillets of beef, 225g each
olive oil
salt and pepper
20 raw langoustines, tails out of
  the shell
2 garlic cloves, chopped
90g butter
juice of 1 lemon, plus 1 lemon,
  quartered
1 tbsp tarragon leaves

This is the posh version and I have used langoustine tails, but you can always get away with prawns, or splash out on lobster. The tarragon and lemon make a big difference to the flavour.

Heat the oven to 180°C (gas 4) and place a large frying pan over a high heat. Rub the meat with olive oil. Add the beef to the pan and season well. Sear on both sides for 5 minutes then transfer to the oven to cook for approximately 6 minutes. The result will be rare. Set aside to rest for 5 minutes while making the sauce.

Take the frying pan and place it back on the stove, adding 2 tsp olive oil. Drop the langoustines into the pan and cook for 2 minutes, then turn and cook for another 2 minutes. Remove the langoustines from the heat and place in a warmed serving dish.

Add the garlic and half the butter to the pan and allow to melt over a medium heat for 1 minute. Add the remaining butter and cook for another 2 minutes, until it begins to brown. Pour in the lemon juice and add the tarragon, then pour the sauce over the langoustines.

Put the steaks on serving plates and spoon the sauce and the tails over. Serve with salad and the lemon wedges.

'GRATIN DAUPHINOISE'

1.4kg baking potatoes
1.2 litres milk
freshly grated nutmeg
sea salt and ground white
   pepper
30g unsalted butter
250ml double cream
115g gruyère cheese, grated
1 garlic clove, halved

Heat the oven to 190°C (gas 5). Thinly slice the potatoes and put them in a large saucepan with the milk, some nutmeg and salt, and half the butter. Bring to the boil, stirring occasionally, and cook until the potatoes are tender, about 10 minutes.

Mix together 100ml cream and half the grated cheese and add this mixture to the potatoes.

Rub the bottom of a baking dish with the garlic and remaining butter. Pour the potatoes in their creamy mixture into the baking dish. Scatter with the remaining cheese and then pour over the last of the cream. Bake for 60-70 minutes, or until the cheese bubbles and browns.

You can either leave the dauphinoise to settle for 10 minutes, then put it in the middle of the table with a big spoon for everyone to help themselves, or do what we do in the restaurant:

Leave the dauphinoise to cool down, then put a baking tray the same size as the dish on top of it and turn it out. Cut the dauphinoise into squares (sit them on baking paper if you like) and reheat them in the oven at 220°C (gas 7) for 5-10 minutes before serving.

'T-BONE STEAK WITH TURNIP & MUSTARD GRATIN'

4 T-bone steaks
vegetable oil
salt and black pepper

turnip gratin
butter, for greasing
500g turnips
250ml double cream
50ml crème fraîche
50ml dijon mustard
100g gruyère cheese, grated

The T-bone is an extraordinary cut. It has to be prepared by a skilled butcher as they need to cut through a rib bone leaving the fillet attached on one side and the sirloin attached on the other.

We tend to serve them quite thin and like that they take only about 8 minutes to cook, but the Italians love them thickly cut, in which case they are known as Toscana. These steaks are far too big for one person (unless they're huge eaters) and they are just grilled.

Heat the oven to 220°C (gas 7) and butter a lasagne dish around 5-7.5cm deep. Peel and slice the turnips and leave them to soak in cold water while you do the rest of the preparation.

Bring the cream to the boil in a saucepan and immediately take the pan off the heat. Stir in the crème fraîche and mustard.

Put a kettle of water on to boil. Drain the turnips and put in a heatproof bowl. Cover with the boiling water and leave to blanch for 2 minutes. Drain well.

Gently mix the cream mixture with the turnips, then pour into the buttered pie dish. Sprinkle with the cheese. Tap the dish so it all packs down and bake for 20 minutes or until really brown on top.

While that's in the oven, cook the steaks. They will need 8 minutes if just a T-bone or 12 minutes for a thick Toscana. Leave a ridged cast-iron plate over a high heat for 10 minutes before you even think about putting the steaks on it. Rub the steaks with oil and season both sides. Open the window so smoke can escape. Place the steaks on the griddle and leave for 2 minutes, then flip and repeat. Cook as long as you need and then leave them to rest. You can put really thick steaks in the oven (still on the griddle) to finish if you like.

Serve with the turnip gratin. T-bones also taste great with gratin dauphinoise (page 142).

'BEEF FOR 100'

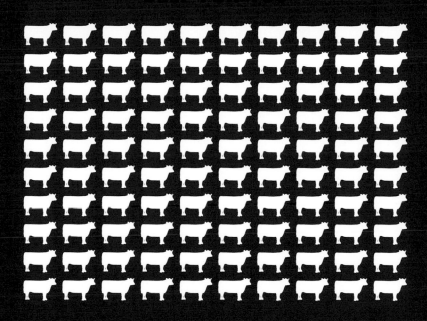

The ritual of a cooking meat on a spit is a boy's thing and it should probably stay that way! It involves getting the biggest piece of meat that you can find, preferably a butt of beef, and cooking the whole thing long and slow; it will take a good six hours. Gas-fired spit roasters can be hired and most companies even take them away dirty and clean them afterwards... result! The best spit roasters have a cover and come with full instructions. The cover is important: the whole joint needs to be enclosed so it can cook gently but with a good amount of heat.

A butt of beef is made up of the rump, the topside, the silverside and shin, all held together by a massive bone. The night before cooking, make up a rub for the outside of the meat. This will never penetrate the whole joint but that's ok because the crisp, salty, herbed exterior is reserved for the master carver and his mates. We call it carver's rights! Mix together a good two handfuls of salt, a handful of black pepper, ten crushed garlic cloves, a good handful of chopped rosemary and 200ml oil and rub the butt all over with the mixture.

Next day you have to impale it. This is a serious business because, as the meat cooks, it will give way and if not secured properly the rod in the middle will be turning and the meat will not. (In Australia, should this happen, we simply say: 'You're stuffed.')
Once that joint starts to turn there is no way you should stop it or it will be well done on one side and raw on the other. Some hire companies provide the meat trussed and ready to rock and roll, or if you tell your butcher what you are doing he will probably put it on the spit for you. Otherwise, just avoid the bone and try to ensure that the spit comes out as far towards the hoof end as possible. I find a couple of big lengths of garden wire really useful for trussing the beef up if it starts to come away.

After six hours of roasting you will have a good 10cm of properly cooked meat. Although the bone acts as a conductor of heat, you will nevertheless need to eat the beef in shifts – but that is part of the joy. As the first keg runs out and you tap the second keg, you have another round of beef. It reminds me of my 21st birthday party.

Okay, now to carve. The best way is to keep the heat on low and stop and start the spit while you carve. Very few gatherings will devour the whole butt and very few people can cook the whole thing all the way through in one go without the exterior drying out (yuk), so expect to leave it to cook for a further hour or so once you get close to the bone.

Simply select a place and start carving the beef from right to left, keeping the knife flat and the slices thin. Remember the crusty outer is reserved for the selected few (it can cause beef wars, so be careful). As you carve, stack the meat on metal trays and keep it hot at the bottom of the spit if the gannets are not quick enough to eat it.

'BEST BREAKFAST BAPS'

500g potatoes, peeled and
  quartered
750g-800g unbleached strong
  flour, plus extra for dusting
4 tsp salt
100g lard, cubed
2 small sachets fast-acting dried
  yeast
2 tsp sugar
2 tsp vegetable oil

If you want to serve homemade baps at your party, it's better to make this recipe nine or ten times rather than try to tackle one gigantic batch. The recipe is easily halved too, but I always make a double lot as I like them toasted the next day with butter, Vegemite and mature cheddar. The baps can be made a few days in advance and then gently warmed if need be; they can also be frozen.

Cook the potatoes in a pot of boiling water until tender. Drain, reserving 250ml of the cooking liquid, and set aside to cool. Put 700g flour and the salt in a mixing bowl and rub in the lard. Add the dried yeast and sugar to the cooled cooking liquid and stir well. Mash the potatoes.

Mix the potatoes into the flour, then add the yeast liquid. Mix in enough of the remaining flour to form a soft dough. Turn the dough out onto a floured surface and knead until smooth and elastic, about 10 minutes. Alternatively, knead the dough in a machine on medium speed for 4 minutes.

Lightly oil a large bowl. Place the dough in the bowl, turning it so that the ball is covered with oil. Cover the bowl with a damp cloth and leave it to rise somewhere warm for about 1½ hours, or until doubled in volume.

Lightly flour two heavy baking sheets. Punch down the dough and turn it out onto a floured surface. Divide into twelve pieces and roll each into a ball. Place the balls on the baking sheets, keeping them evenly spaced. Cover with a tea towel and leave to rise until puffy, about 40 minutes.

Heat the oven to 200°C (gas 6). Use a rolling pin to gently flatten each ball into a 10cm circle. Sprinkle with flour and bake for 20 minutes, or until the rolls are golden brown on top and sound hollow when tapped on the base.

'DOUBLE-CUT PORTERHOUSE, FRIED SALSIFY & BEARNAISE SAUCE'

4 double-cut porterhouse
   steaks, about 400g each
vegetable oil

fried salsify
1kg salsify
squeeze of lemon juice
50g plain flour
1 egg
20ml milk
3 handfuls fresh breadcrumbs
salt and pepper

to serve
Béarnaise sauce (page 131)
1 bunch of watercress

This is a serious cards-night dinner for people with really big appetites. A double-cut porterhouse or sirloin is rarely seen but it is really worth it because, when cooked, the outside is crisp and salty and buttery while the inside is still rare, almost blue, so you get to eat the steak at every stage from well done to rare. I think that's a great way to understand how you really like your meat cooked. As I've already said, there's nothing wrong with liking your steak any way you want, as long as it's not dry – otherwise you might as well eat a chunk of cardboard soaked in gravy.

Peel the salsify and keep it in a bowl of water with some lemon juice to stop it going brown. Bring a large saucepan of water to the boil. Cut the salsify into pieces 10cm long and add them to the boiling water. Cook for about 15 minutes until tender, then drain the salsify and spread it out on paper towel to cool.

Lay out three wide but not-too-deep bowls, one with the flour, one with the egg and milk beaten together, and one with the breadcrumbs. Dust the salsify in the flour, then dip it in the egg mixture, then roll in the breadcrumbs until evenly coated. Leave in the fridge until you are ready to proceed.

Heat a frying pan until hot. Rub the steaks with oil, cook them, then remove them from the pan and set aside to rest. Add 100ml oil to the pan and fry the salsify – it's a bit like cooking sausages. When the salsify is done, drain it briefly on some paper towel and serve with the steaks, watercress and sauce.

'FILLET OF BEEF, BONE MARROW & PARMESAN'

4 slices white bread
30ml vegetable oil
4 fillets of beef, 225g each
4 pieces of tall long bone and
   bone marrow (optional)

sauce

500ml good chicken stock
50g parmesan cheese, grated
100g raw bone marrow, diced
15 rocket leaves
salt and pepper

In my life there have been few dishes that I can call truly my own – this, however, is one. I devised and tested and cooked and played with this before we opened Mezzo in 1995 and it sat proud on the menu the whole time I was there.

Heat the oven to 180°C (gas 4).

Cut a round disc from each slice of bread to make a crouton approximately the size of the beef fillet. Warm the oil in a frying pan and fry the bread until crisp on both sides. Remove and drain on paper towel.

Drain the pan of oil and return it to a high heat. When hot, add the fillets of beef and season well. Sear on both sides for 5 minutes then transfer the meat to the oven to cook for approximately 5 minutes. The result will be rare fillets of beef. If using the pieces of bone and marrow, put them on a roasting tray and roast them for 5 minutes.

Remove the beef from the oven and leave to rest for 5 minutes while making the sauce.

Bring the stock to the boil in a saucepan. Whisk in the parmesan, then the diced bone marrow. Do not let the sauce return to the boil. Add the rocket, stirring until wilted, then season to taste.

Place a crouton on each serving plate. Sit the fillet of beef on top and garnish each one with a piece of bone marrow, if using. Pour the sauce over and serve.

'CLASSIC CHATEAUBRIAND'

1 handful white peppercorns
1 head of the fillet, 1kg
50ml vegetable oil
50g butter
2 tbsp cognac
5 tbsp dry white wine
5 tbsp game stock
150ml double cream
salt

Roasting a chunk of fillet to lay on the table with a great sauce is very cool and always impresses! I like the peppercorns but you don't have to use them – do it plain if you like and eat hot or cold. The head of the fillet is big and has a line of sinew running through it. You can replace the game stock with some good veal stock (page 24) if necessary.

Heat the oven to 230°C (gas 8). Crush the peppercorns using a pestle and mortar or an empty bottle and press them into the meat so that it is 'breadcrumbed' all over.

Heat the oil and butter in a roasting tin, add the meat and roast for 20 minutes, basting frequently. Remove from the oven and transfer the meat to a serving dish – keep it hot by covering it with a sheet of buttered greaseproof paper.

Drain the cooking fat from the tin, then place over a high heat. Deglaze the pan with the cognac, then add the white wine, bring to a boil and let it reduce by half. Add the stock, return to the boil, add the cream and let the sauce reduce, stirring all the time.

Pour in the juices that have run out of the joint. Stir and taste for seasoning, adding salt if necessary. Don't on any account add pepper!

Carve the meat on a big platter and cut them into 12 pieces. Coat the beef with the hot sauce, including all the peppercorns that have fallen off during cooking.

'STEAK TARTARE'

750g beef fillet tails
1 large bunch parsley, chopped
salt and pepper
65ml Worcestershire sauce
100ml tomato sauce
100g capers, finely chopped
150g shallots, finely chopped
4 egg yolks
Tabasco sauce, to serve

The great steak tartare can only be made with one cut of beef and that is the tail of the fillet. If anyone tells you different they are WRONG!! Also the meat should never be put through a mincer unless it is a little hand-operated one, but trust me you will waste too much. Really the meat should be chopped and you will find that using a large chopping knife is a great way to get rid of the frustrations of the day. You need about 180g meat per serving. The other ingredients give the dish life and I believe everyone should mix their own tartare at the table as we all like it different, don't we? I believe that this dish is best served with toast and chips – but straw chips with lots of salt – and preferably eaten on a good black run in a sunny ski resort – that should get the digestive juices working! Oh by the way – if you grill the mixture you will have a good spicy hamburger.

Cut the meat into matchstick-thin strips, then bundle them up, turn them around 180 degrees and cut into little cubes. Start chopping the meat and continue until it eventually forms into a ball on the board.

Mix the meat with some of the parsley, some pepper, Worcestershire sauce and a little tomato sauce. Spoon it on to serving plates and shape into a mound. The remaining ingredients should be arranged around the meat, and an egg yolk placed in the centre of each serving. This allows everyone to add and mix and play and season – that's half the fun.

Tip Taking the mixture straight from the fridge, making sure it is very cold, will help the meat bind and stay good and moist.

'THE GREAT BURGER'

So you want to know the secret of a great beef burger? You want it to be big and juicy even when it is cooked well done. There are a couple of tricks. A good burger needs fat. I try and use mince with 40 per cent fat – it sounds a lot but you need it to keep the meat moist while grilling. My other secret is to use Chinese oyster sauce instead of salt. Salt makes the mixture dry and crumbly because it draws the water from the meat.

Mix the beef, onion and parsley together in a bowl. Add the oyster sauce and ketchup, then the egg yolk. Mix well and knead until thoroughly combined. Divide the mixture into six equal portions and roll each one into a large ball. Place them in the fridge and, if possible, leave them to chill for a good hour.

To cook, either have your barbecue good and hot with coals glowing, or heat a griddle over a medium heat. Do not add oil.

Place the burgers on the barbecue or griddle plate and leave for a few minutes until the edges start to colour. Slide a fish slice under each burger and turn them over. Repeat on the other side.

Turn the burgers again but, if using a barbecue, move the burgers to the side or another area where it is slightly cooler; if using a griddle plate reduce the heat underneath. Leave the burgers to cook for a good 15 minutes if you would like them well done.

Serve your burgers with whatever you want. At Smiths we top them with a piece of grilled bacon and a slice of good-quality cheddar and put them under the grill for a few minutes until the cheese has melted. We toast the buns and spread them with mayonnaise, not butter. Cooked salad is disgusting so any salad should be served separately, along with mustard and a wally. You've got to have a wally on the side!

1.5kg fatty minced beef
2 red onions, diced
1 large handful flat-leaf parsley, chopped
2 tbsp oyster sauce
2 tbsp tomato ketchup
1 egg yolk

'THE ROAST'

Roast beef is the one thing I remember as a kid that would have everybody wearing a smile – not just because it smells so amazing when it is cooking, or that it arguably makes the best gravy of any roast meat, or that there will be big bones to chew.

This really can be straightforward, but so many of us get it so wrong. To me the best roast beef ever in the world is a British fore rib, preferably matured on the bone for 28 days after slaughter, and taken from a Dexter rare breed heifer after one calf.... controversy. But let's be honest, we can't all be that specific, so what are we looking for?

Well the fore rib is, as the name suggests, at the fore of the beast. Those of you lucky enough to eat a t-bone steak are nearly there. A fore rib looks like something from The Flintstones – think of an oversized rack of lamb. It's a large hunk of meat attached to a bone. Each bone will serve at least two people and a single bone fore rib steak grilled is a côte de boeuf. The biggest hunk you will get is a five-bone rib and, wow, is that exciting! About 6kg in weight, it has an additional large bone, the chine, attached. To my mind this joint should be what everyone cooks at Easter.

The rib needs marbling – marbling is just fat that is in the meat. It slowly disappears (or renders) as it cooks, keeping the beef moist. Under-mature beef with no fat through the meat will be a dry and tasteless disappointment and you will get little yield from it. Ask your butcher for a short-bone rib: you don't want the brisket on unless you are a good butcher yourself. The layer of fat should be white with a touch of yellow – too much yellow and it will taste very grassy and the meat will not have a good structure. The beef should also be well marbled and the marbling white: if it is yellow, just say no!

I like to salt the fat 12 hours before the joint goes in the oven as I like crispy beef fat. To do this, take the rib and turn it so the fat is sitting up facing you. Criss-cross the fat with a sharp knife, being careful to cut only into the fat, don't go too deep. Then make a 50/50 mixture of chopped rosemary and salt and add a good amount of pepper. Rub a handful of seasoning over the fat, then turn the meat over and rub it into the rib bones and flesh. Put the joint in the fridge, have a glass of red, and go to bed.

The next day, heat the oven to 180°C (gas 4). For each rib (or 1.5kg) I allow about 45 minutes cooking time so a five-boner will take about 3 ¾ hours. That means you will get a well-done outside, medium just inside, medium rare meat then, at the centre, rare beef. After cooking, the beef must be left to relax for a good 20 minutes before it is carved. Put it on a board with the fat facing the carver and the bow of the bone pointing away.

I like to roast my meat with good spuds, which should be placed under the joint 1 hour 20 minutes before serving. That allows you to take them out and keep them warm in a serving dish, then pour most of the fat off and use it to make the Yorkshire puds.

You should be left with a roasting tray containing lots of bits. Now it's time to make the gravy. My nanna's gravy recipe is very special to me. From the age of six I stood on a stool and made it; I loved all the stirring and bubbling and the experience of being over the heat of the oven.

You will need a little fat to get this gravy right, so keep about a tablespoon of it in the roasting tray and put it over a low heat. Sprinkle in about 2 tablespoons of flour and stir really well – the heat will give it colour, and the flour will become like brown breadcrumbs. If an edge starts to burn you might have to move the tray off the heat, or shuffle it around, but do that and it will all be ok.

Add a little salt, turn the heat up to medium and pour in 300ml water (cold is fine). Stir and stir and stir – as the heat builds the lumps will disappear. As you boil the gravy it will get thick.

Then you add some more water, boil again and it will get thick. Then add some more water, boil again and it will get thick. Then add some more water and boil again until the gravy is the thickness you like.

Taste it and I bet you an Australian dollar (that's what I used to get paid to do the washing up after lunch) that the gravy does not need seasoning and it will be the best you have ever eaten. It takes time but, boy, it is good. PS it is good cold with cold roast potatoes too.

Tip The bones in a joint of meat conduct the heat and therefore help to cook it more evenly than a boneless cut. They also stop the shrinkage, and so your yield is far better when cooking on the bone. If you are going to cook a joint off the bone, then sear it well before roasting. Rub it with oil, salt and pepper and place in a large, heavy pan over a high heat, turning so that it is well-coloured on all sides. This will help keep the juices inside.

'MY CHRISTMAS ROAST BEEF WITH MUSTARD CRUST'

5kg five-bone rib of beef, trimmed
100ml oil
salt and pepper
4 carrots, peeled and halved

mustard crust

50g butter
2 large onions, diced
300g fresh white breadcrumbs
300g wholegrain or other mustard
3 eggs

Ask your butcher to trim the beef, remove the chine bone (which is the flat bone attached to the rib) and to clean the bones ready for roasting, but keep the trimmings. The fat is great for roasting the potatoes and if you ask the butcher to mince the remaining trim it makes great meatballs for nibbles.

You can use any type of mustard for this recipe. I like the speckled effect and flavour of wholegrain, but if you decide on English mustard be careful not to overdo it.

First thing in the morning, remove the beef from the fridge to allow it to come up to room temperature. Score the fat on the top of the rib well – this will stop it curling. Rub the joint all over with oil, then season with salt and pepper.

Heat the oven to 220°C (gas 7).

To make the crust (which can be done the day before serving), heat the butter in a pan and sweat the onions so they are tender but not coloured. Tip them into a big bowl and add the breadcrumbs, mustard, eggs and 200ml water. Stir well to make a paste.

Spread the paste evenly over the beef, leaving the ends uncovered. Cover the crust with a sheet of well-greased foil. Place the carrots in a large roasting tray and sit the beef on them. Roast in the oven for 2½ hours, removing the foil for the final hour. When done, take the beef from the oven and leave it to rest for 20 minutes while you make a gravy (page 33 or 153).

'RED CABBAGE'

100g butter
5 rashers smoked bacon,
   chopped
2 red cabbages, cored and sliced
4 Granny Smith apples, peeled,
   cored and sliced
100g raisins
rind of ½ orange, chopped
2 cinnamon sticks
200g brown sugar
salt and pepper
300ml red wine
50ml red wine vinegar

Place a heavy-based pan, preferably cast-iron, over a high heat and melt the butter. Add the bacon, fry until slightly coloured, then remove from the heat and set aside.

Lay a quarter of the sliced cabbage in the base of the pan. Top with a quarter of the apples, a quarter of the raisins, plus some bacon, orange rind, cinnamon and brown sugar. Season with salt and pepper then repeat the layers until all the ingredients are used.

Set the pan over high heat and add the wine and vinegar. Bring to the boil and cook for 3-4 minutes. Cover, reduce the heat as low as possible and cook for 1 hour to 1 hour 50 minutes, until tender. Do not stir the cabbage at any stage; ensure that the lid is sealed well but check the liquid every 20 minutes to ensure that it does not evaporate too quickly – if it does, top up with water.

'YORKSHIRE PUDDINGS'

8 eggs
600ml milk
½ tsp salt
500g plain flour
3 tbsp dripping

Heat the oven to 220°C (gas 7). Beat the eggs with the milk and salt. Sieve the flour twice to aerate it, then beat the flour into the milk mixture to make a batter. You can sieve the batter if you like.

Place the Yorkshire tray in the oven until hot. Add a good amount of dripping to each indentation and heat until the fat is smoking.

This is where you must be careful as the fat is very hot: ladle some of the batter into each of the indentations so that they are nearly full, then return the tray to the oven. Reduce the heat to 200°C (gas 6) and cook for 15 minutes.

'THE BEST ROAST POTATOES'

20 large potatoes
250ml beef dripping or lard

Who said there was only one way to roast a potato? Many of us have been merrily popping potatoes in the oven on a high heat with a little oil for years and doing fine; in fact I was one of those people, until I found out there was more to it than that and there was a way I could get a crisper potato – and quicker!

Heat the oven to 220°C (gas 7). Peel the potatoes and cut them in half, or quarters if they are huge. Put them in a pot large enough to hold them all. Boil the kettle and cover the potatoes with the boiling water. Cook over a high heat for 5 minutes.

Remove from the heat and drain well. Put the potatoes back in the pot over a low heat to dry them out, shaking the pot – but not too vigorously or they will be damaged.

Heat the dripping in a large baking dish in the oven for a good 10 minutes so it's really hot. Add the potatoes, coat them in the fat and place in the oven – wherever you have space, but preferably not at the bottom. Cook for 20 minutes, then turn the potatoes over and return to the oven for a further 40 minutes, until they are golden brown and crisp. Drain off the fat and serve.

'CLASSIC BEEF WELLINGTON WITH HONEY PARSNIPS'

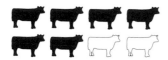

15g dried ceps

1-1.4kg beef fillet, trimmed

salt and pepper

50g butter

2 shallots, chopped

2 garlic cloves, chopped

225g flat mushrooms, finely
   chopped

2 tsp chopped fresh thyme

170g chicken liver pâté

160g parma ham, sliced

flour, for dusting

375g puff pastry

1 egg, beaten

honey parsnips

900g parsnips, peeled

2 tbsp oil

50g butter

2 tbsp clear honey

I don't care what anyone says – a Beef Wellington is the holy grail to any carnivore. It's one of those dishes that has been done so badly at big functions that people have sort of given up on it. But this is so good. Although the recipe is for six to eight people, four could devour it no trouble at all.

Put the dried mushrooms in a heatproof bowl and cover with 100ml boiling water from the kettle. Leave to rehydrate for 30 minutes, then drain, reserving the liquor. Chop the mushrooms and set them and the liquor aside.

Season the beef all over with salt and pepper. Melt half the butter in a large frying pan over a medium heat. When foaming, put the fillet in the pan and brown all over for 4-5 minutes, taking care not to burn the butter. Put the beef on a plate and set aside to cool.

Melt the remaining butter in a separate frying pan. Add the shallots and cook for 1 minute. Add the ceps and garlic, then the reserved liquor and the flat mushrooms. Increase the heat and cook until the mushrooms are dry. Season and add the thyme, then set aside to cool.

Put the pâté in a bowl and beat until smooth. Add the mushroom mixture and stir until thoroughly combined. Taste and adjust the seasoning as necessary.

Transfer the cold beef fillet to a board and use a palette knife to spread half the mushroom mixture evenly over one side of the meat. Take a sheet of cling film and lay half the parma ham on it so that the slices overlap. Lay the fillet mushroom-side down on the ham and spread the remaining mushroom mixture over the beef. Wrap the rest of the parma ham, also overlapping, over the top. Wrap the whole lot in cling film and chill.

Heat the oven to 220°C (gas 7). Cut one-third of the pastry from the block and roll it out to a sheet 3mm thick and 2.5cm larger than the base of the beef. Transfer to a baking sheet, prick well with a fork and bake for 12-15 minutes, until brown and crisp. Allow the pastry to cool, then trim it to the size of the beef.

Take the beef from the fridge and unwrap it. Brush the beef all over with some of the beaten egg and place it on the cooked pastry.

Roll out the remaining pastry to a rectangle about 30 x 35cm. Use this to cover the beef, tucking the ends under and sealing the edges. Brush with the rest of the beaten egg. Place the Wellington on a baking sheet and cook for 40 minutes for rare to medium rare, and 45 minutes for medium.

Meanwhile, halve the parsnips lengthways, or if very large cut them into quarters. Trim out any woody centres. Sit a roasting tray on the stove and add the oil and butter. Fry the parsnips over a high heat until golden brown on all sides, then transfer to the oven and roast for 20 minutes, turning occasionally.

Take the parsnips from the oven. Drizzle the honey over them and stir carefully until they are well coated. Continue roasting for about 5 minutes so that the parsnips are tender and sweet.

Remove the Wellington from the oven and leave to stand for 10 minutes before carving. Put the parsnips in a large serving dish and spoon some of the honey glaze over the top to finish.

'MINCED BEEF WELLINGTON'

1kg minced beef

200g onions, diced

1 handful chopped sage leaves

1 handful chopped parsley

2 garlic cloves, crushed

salt and pepper

100g tomato paste

3 eggs

300g puff pastry

100g pâté, your choice

I have to include this recipe. When I was a kid we could not afford fillet to make beef Wellington but my nanna would do this little number, which is really a meat loaf in puff pastry. I still like it a lot. If you've got picky kids, take out the pâté. You can also use the mince mixture here to make meat loaf – just put it in a tin and bake for 40 minutes or until the top is crisp.

Mix the beef with the onion, herbs, garlic and lots of seasoning. In a bowl, combine the tomato paste with 100ml water and whisk in two of the eggs. Add the egg mixture to the beef and beat with an electric mixer for 5 minutes.

Heat the oven to 200°C (gas 6). Shape the meat into a large sausage, place on a roasting tray and cook in the oven for 20 minutes. Strain off and reserve the pan juices and set them and the meat aside to cool.

Roll out the pastry to a large rectangle about 3mm thick. Beat the remaining egg with a little water and brush over the top of the pastry. Place the meat in the middle and roll the pastry over the meat. Cover with the pâté (your choice this one).

Place on a roasting tray and return to the oven for 30 minutes. Shortly before serving, reheat the pan juices ready to serve with the Wellington, plus some mashed potatoes and tomato sauce.

'VIETNAMESE GRILLED SIRLOIN'

4 minute steaks, or sirloin steaks
   bashed flat
2 spring onions, shredded
1 tsp sesame seeds

sauce
1 tbsp rice wine vinegar
1 red chilli, chopped
25ml fish sauce
juice of 1 lime
1 carrot, peeled and grated
1 garlic clove, chopped
1 knob ginger, peeled and
   chopped
30g sugar

garnish
1 Thai shallot, chopped
1 garlic clove, chopped
1 tbsp sugar
1 tsp fish sauce
ground pepper
12 mint leaves, chopped
1 handful Thai basil
1 handful chopped coriander
2 snake beans, chopped

The minute steak is simply that – a steak that takes just a minute to cook. I prefer to use sirloin as it has more flavour and I believe that bashing a piece of fillet is fundamentally a waste of money.

The secret to cooking a minute steak lies in the heat of the griddle, frying pan or coals. You must get them really, really, really bloody hot and the oil must go on the steak and not on the grill.

To make the sauce, heat the vinegar in a saucepan and add the chopped chilli. Allow to cool slightly, then add the fish sauce, lime juice, carrot, garlic and ginger. Add the sugar and 350ml water and stir until the sugar has dissolved. Set aside.

Combine all the ingredients for the garnish in a bowl, then toss with a little of the sauce. Spread on serving plates.

Grill the beef for 30 seconds on each side, then place it on top of the vegetable garnish. Sprinkle the spring onions and sesame seeds on top before serving.

'ROAST SIRLOIN WITH OYSTER SAUCE & GINGER'

2kg piece sirloin, with its layer
  of fat still on
2 tsp Chinese five-spice powder
1 tsp caster sugar
salt and pepper
vegetable oil

sauce
300ml chicken stock
1 garlic clove
70ml Chinese oyster sauce
3 spring onions
1 good thumb-sized piece ginger,
  peeled and skin reserved
½ bunch coriander

The night before if possible, take the sirloin and score the fat in a criss-cross pattern. Mix together the five-spice, sugar, a good teaspoon of ground pepper and a good amount of salt. Rub this into the fat of the beef and leave overnight.

Next day, heat the oven to 200°C (gas 6). Take some oil and rub it forcefully over the meat. Set a griddle pan over a high heat and leave it for about 15 minutes to get hot – very important.

Place the meat fat-side down on the griddle and leave to shimmer. The fat will start to melt and the spices start to cook. Don't touch it – just leave it. If you have scored the fat well you have no worries at all, if you have not then the meat will curl and toughen.

After 5 minutes when your kitchen is full of smoke (good reason to do this outside on a barbie), turn the meat over and transfer it to the oven. A 2kg piece of sirloin will need 25 minutes. Bring it out and leave it to rest, or even cool for serving later.

Meanwhile, combine the stock, garlic and oyster sauce in a large saucepan along with the trimmings of the spring onions, the ginger peel, and the stalks and roots of the coriander (reserve the leaves). Bring to a boil then turn the heat off and leave to infuse for about 5 minutes.

Cut the ginger into the thinnest slices and from those slice the thinnest strips. Slice the spring onions, keeping the white portion separate from the green. Mix the green spring onion with the coriander leaves and set aside for garnishing.

Strain the flavourings from the stock and return the liquid to the pan. Bring it back to the boil and add the shredded ginger and the white parts of the spring onion. Get it off that heat.

Sauce made. Beef cooked. Now you do what you want!

Tip The stock, once flavoured, is also good for cooking Asian vegetables like pak choy, green mustard and Chinese broccoli – all of which taste best served hot.

'ROAST RIB OF BEEF WITH HORSERADISH BREAD PUDDING'

3kg rolled rib of beef off the
  bone
20g salt
10g pepper
150ml vegetable oil or dripping
20 large potatoes, peeled and
  halved

**horseradish bread
  puddings**

1 small loaf white bread
butter, for greasing
4 eggs
100ml soured cream
100g creamed horseradish
200ml chicken stock
salt and pepper

I would love to give a recipe for four but I can't – a whole rib of beef roasted slowly is just a thing so beautiful it would be hard to make it tiny. The pudding is the same as a bread and butter pudding but with horseradish added. It is very delicious but must be crisp on top.

Heat the oven to 200°C (gas 6). Rub the rolled rib with salt and pepper and then a good 60ml of vegetable oil. Put the roasting tray in the oven with the rest of the oil in it and leave for 10 minutes to get hot.

Add the potatoes to the roasting tray and place the beef in the centre. Turn the beef once and shake the potatoes so they are covered with oil. Return the roasting tray to the oven and leave it without opening the door for 30 minutes.

Take the crusts off the loaf of bread and keep them to feed the ducks – you will need to go for a walk after this dinner. Slice the bread and cut each piece into triangles. Grease a ceramic baking dish with butter.

Mix together the eggs, soured cream, horseradish, stock and some salt and pepper. Lay the bread in the dish with the points sticking up, then pour over the egg mixture. Place in the oven for 40 minutes, or until crisp on top.

After the beef has been cooking for a total of 1 hour 10 minutes, take it and the spuds out of the oven and use the pan juices to make a gravy (page 33 or 153). Serve the beef with the pudding, plus some green beans and extra creamed horseradish.

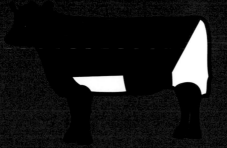

SALT BEEF
BRESAOLA & PASTRAMI

Salting and smoking beef are very old techniques devised to cope with seasonal gluts of fresh meat. Cattle would feed on grass all summer then, as the cold came, fatten up on the grain that was left after harvest. Once killed, the mass of fresh meat meant people either had to eat the lot or preserve it. The seafaring Dutch even swapped Manhattan in order to secure supplies of nutmeg, a natural preservative used in curing, ensuring their ships had good supplies of preserved meat. For me, salting and curing a piece of beef like brisket is a real treat. Boiled with carrots and served hot with mustard and parsley sauce, it is perfect comfort food. At the same time, sitting and eating a simple salt beef sandwich and having that big pickle (known as a wally) is also a great treat.

'SALT BEEF'

3-4kg piece boneless silverside, topside or brisket, trimmed of any fat
4.5 litres boiling water
1.2kg sea salt, or 1kg salt plus 200g saltpetre
600g soft dark brown sugar
50g coriander seeds
24 juniper berries
12 peppercorns
12 allspice berries
4 cloves
2 cardamom pods
1.5 litres ice-cold water
6 bay leaves

Making salt beef (known as corned beef where I come from) is not something many of us will do, but should you want to this is how to go about it. The thickness of the beef will determine how long it stays in the brine: a full topside, round like a football, will take 2 weeks, but a small book-shaped brisket about 4 days. Saltpetre would ideally be included but due to the problems with terrorism you may not be able to buy it (though try asking your butcher). The French have something called sel rouge which, if you can get it, works as well. As long as you are making salt beef just for home use and not for sale, and you can keep the meat refrigerated, saltpetre is not essential however it is a great preservative.

Under no circumstances should the meat have bone in, on or near it, as this will rot rather than pickle. Have the boiling water ready in a pot. Add the salt and sugar and bring back to the boil.

Meanwhile, heat a large frying pan until almost smoking and throw in all the spices. Take off the heat and let the spices toast, shaking the pan a few times to ensure they do so evenly. Tie the spices in a piece of muslin or old tea towel then drop into the boiling water. Keep the pot boiling for 15 minutes to dissolve the salt and sugar and make the liquid very salty. Turn the heat off, pour the ice-cold water into the pot and leave to cool.

Add the meat and bay leaves to the brine, making sure the meat is completely immersed, and cover tightly. Leave in the fridge for the time needed (see above). You can turn the meat every so often but try just to let it bob about in the pickling liquid.

Once cured, it will last a few days in the fridge and – if you have used saltpetre – a lot longer.

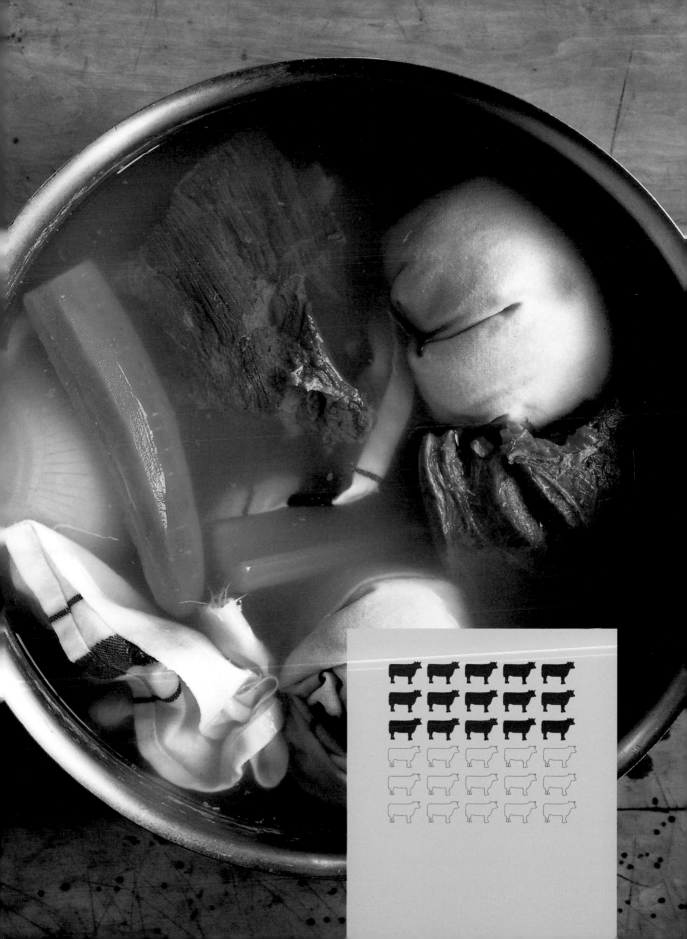

'SALT BEEF, PEASE PUDDING & STUFF'

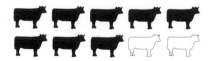

pease pudding
200g marrowfat peas

1 tsp bicarbonate of soda

50g butter

salt and pepper

1 egg

salt beef
2kg salt beef (page 166)

2 large onions, peeled and
halved

2 large carrots, peeled and
halved

1 celery stick

12 peppercorns

2 bay leaves

2 parsley stalks

mustard sauce
60g butter

60g plain flour

600ml milk

2 tbsp French mustard

potatoes
8-12 large potatoes, peeled and
halved

1 knob of butter

The great thing about large hunks of preserved meat is that you can eat them over a period of time. In the modern world there's a tendency for people to look at recipes that only last one meal when the real way to save time in the kitchen is to cook recipes that last three or four meals. Remember the beef has already been cooked by the salting process, so all you are really doing here is getting it hot.

The night before serving, soak the peas in loads of water. Next day, drain off the water and rinse the peas three times. Then put them in a saucepan, cover with water and add the bicarb, stirring well. Bring to the boil and cook for a good hour, until tender, topping up the water so the peas are always covered.

While the peas are cooking, start on the beef. In a large pot, put the salt beef, vegetables, peppercorns, bay leaves and parsley stalks. Cover with water and bring to a rolling simmer. Cook for at least two hours, periodically topping up the water.

Once the peas are cooked, put them in a food processor with the butter, lots of salt and pepper, and a little of their cooking liquor. Blend until nearly smooth, then add the egg and mix well. Taste and adjust the seasoning if necessary.

Take a pudding cloth, tea towel or (something I like to use) an old clean pillow case and lay it in a bowl. Spoon the pea mush into the middle then tie it up in a bundle with string. Put the whole thing in the pot with the beef as it continues cooking.

To make the sauce, melt the butter over a low heat. Stir in the flour to make a roux. Add the milk, stirring well until smooth. Bring to the boil, then add the mustard, a little salt and remove from the heat. Now I like to blend it to aerate the sauce and make

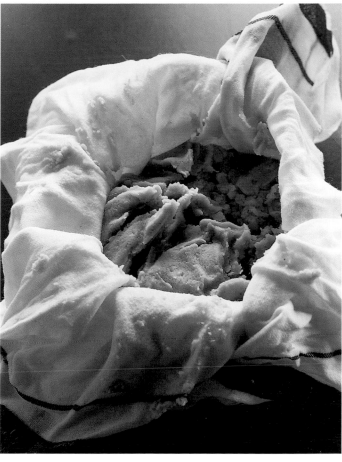

it really silky – you can do this with a hand blender or a food processor, otherwise just beat it really hard or strain it through a sieve. Return the sauce to the pan and reheat it, adding a little of the cooking liquor from the salt beef.

About 20 minutes before the beef is going to be ready, put the potatoes in a pan of cold water with some salt. Add some of the cooking liquor from the salt beef, then bring to the boil and cook for 20 minutes. Remove the pan from the heat and drain the potatoes. Put them in a bowl with a good amount of butter and cover with cling film to keep warm while you get everything else ready to serve.

To serve, slice the salt beef and put the mustard sauce in a jug. Open the pease pudding and serve it in spoonfuls with the salt beef and potatoes.

'BREAD SAUCE'

500ml milk
1 medium onion, peeled and halved
6 black peppercorns
2 cloves
1 small blade mace, or 1 pinch nutmeg
sea salt
120g fresh white breadcrumbs
30g butter

I was a late starter where bread sauce is concerned; it wasn't until I landed on the shores of Blighty that I discovered it. Served with all sorts of salted meats, poultry and game, it is truly delicious.

Put the milk in a saucepan, then add the onion, peppercorns, cloves, mace or nutmeg and some salt. Set the pan over a medium heat and heat the milk to simmering point – try not to let it boil, but if you do, add a little cold milk. Cook for 5 minutes then remove the pan from the heat and leave to infuse, preferably for 1 hour (but it can be done in 15 minutes).

Take a clean saucepan and put the breadcrumbs in it. Pour the infused milk through a strainer and into the pan, then leave to soak for 5 minutes. Put the pan over a medium heat and cook the sauce slowly for 10 minutes, stirring often.

Stir in the butter to give a thick sauce with some body – a bit like porridge. If it is too thick, add a little more milk; if too thin, continue cooking the sauce until enough liquid has evaporated to give the desired consistency.

'PARSLEY SAUCE'

50g butter
50g plain flour
200ml milk
300ml broth from cooking salt beef (page 168)
1 tbsp English mustard powder
salt and pepper
1 handful parsley, stalks trimmed

Another great sauce to serve with salt beef.

In a saucepan, melt the butter, stir in the flour and cook over a low heat for 2 minutes.

Mix the milk and broth, add the mustard and stir to dissolve. Season as necessary – it shouldn't need much, maybe a little salt. Gradually add the liquid to the flour paste, stirring constantly, to avoid lumps. Bring to the boil and cook for 5 minutes.

Rip up the parsley and add. Using a stick blender or a food processor, blitz until the sauce turns green. Pour over your salt beef and vegetables.

'SALT BEEF HASH, SPINACH & FRIED EGGS'

250g salt beef
3 large cooked jacket potatoes, peeled
salt and pepper
100g butter
4 eggs
100g baby spinach leaves

For brunch I don't reckon it gets much better than this. Equal amounts of grated salt beef (some people even use Spam) and potatoes fried in butter... oh yeah! You can make this posh by cooking it in little pans and serving with poached eggs, or you can do it in one big pan and then serve it scooped out with fried eggs.

Grate the salt beef and your peeled baked spuds using a cheese grater. Mix the two together, season with lots of pepper and maybe some salt, then knead the mixture really well.

Drop half the butter into a nonstick frying pan and, as it starts to melt, add half the hash mixture. Give it a stir and let it colour, then give another stir and let it colour some more, and then again so that it is all hot. Press down on the hash so it flattens like a thick pancake.

Meanwhile, poach or fry the eggs as you prefer.

Cover the hash with half the spinach leaves, let it cook for a few minutes, then fold one half of the hash over like an omelette and flip it out onto a plate. Keep it warm while you repeat the cooking process with the rest of the hash mixture. Cut each batch in half and serve with the eggs.

'SALT BEEF SANDWICH, PICKLES & MUSTARD MAYONNAISE'

2 thick slices soft rye bread
mayonnaise
dijon mustard
hot salt beef
big pickled gherkin

In the Jewish tradition, you can't eat dairy products and beef together, so remember to spread mayo on the bread instead of butter.

Make your sandwich in the usual way but, instead of butter, spread the bread with the mayonnaise, then add a stripe of mustard.

Slice the hot boiled beef – not too thick – and pile it onto the bread. You can then either slice the pickle and put it inside the sandwich, or serve it on the side, or both.

'BRESAOLA'

4kg topside beef

marinade
750g coarse sea salt
1 bottle cheap red wine
1 bottle cheap white wine
1 large bunch rosemary
12 bay leaves
24 cloves
3 garlic cloves, crushed
40 black peppercorns
12 dried red chillies
4 strips orange peel

This classic Italian cured meat is made from the topside. The meat is first marinated then hung to dry, which takes 40 days. You can easily buy ready-made bresaola from Italian delis and supermarkets, then serve the following dishes with it, but I do feel that we should all preserve a foodstuff once in our lives. This recipe will give you three or four decent-sized pieces that will last a family for 6 months. If you want to make less, simply reduce the volume of ingredients to suit 1kg beef, but it's not really worth making less.

Trim the beef, removing the fat and sinews so that you have a number of nuts of meat rather than one big hunk. Combine all the ingredients for the marinade in a large non-corrosive dish big enough to hold all the meat and then some. Add the meat, cover and leave for 2 weeks in the back of the fridge.

After a fortnight, cut squares of muslin big enough to wrap each hunk of meat. Take the meat from the marinade and wrap each piece with cloth, then bundle it with some string, tying it like a present. Hang the meat somewhere cool that allows the air to circulate, such as the back shed in winter. Leave for 2 more weeks, checking every so often that the bundles of beef are not touching each other otherwise the air won't circulate freely around them.

To serve the bresaola, slice it very thinly. Sprinkle with olive oil and season with pepper and chives. Garnish with wedges of lemon and eat with big hunks of bread.

'BRESAOLA WITH CELERIAC & MUSTARD DRESSING'

1 large celeriac root
1 large handful chopped flat-leaf
  parsley
32 slices bresaola
20ml olive oil
4 lemon wedges

dressing

2 tbsp dijon mustard
1 tbsp champagne vinegar
½ tbsp caster sugar
2 tbsp vegetable oil
½ tbsp hazelnut oil
120ml single cream

Celeriac rémoulade is a very quick but also very classic salad for serving with cured meats and fish. This is good with a boiled egg on top, too.

Make the dressing first. In a bowl, whisk together the mustard, vinegar, sugar and both oils until combined. Add the single cream and whisk gently for 20 seconds just to incorporate – if you beat it too much it will go thick and split and be nasty.

Peel and slice the celeriac, then cut it into thin strips – as thin as linguine. Alternatively, you can shred it on a mandolin. Gently mix the dressing with the celeriac and parsley.

Lay the bresaola out on four serving plates. Wind the celeriac strips around a fork as if you were eating spaghetti and place them in the centre of the bresaola. Sprinkle each plate with olive oil and serve with a wedge of lemon.

'BRESAOLA & MOZZARELLA PIZZA'

tomato sauce
60ml olive oil
1 onion, diced
1 garlic clove, crushed
1 tsp sea salt
1 tsp ground black pepper
700g good-quality canned
   chopped tomatoes

dough
250ml warm water
10g fresh yeast
½ tsp sugar
375g 'oo' (doppio zero) flour,
   plus extra for dusting
1 tsp salt
1 tbsp olive oil, plus extra for
   greasing

topping
36 slices bresaola
1 large ball mozzarella

I don't know anybody who doesn't like pizza and this is the quickest and the best dough I know of to make a truly thin and tasty crisp pizza.

For the tomato sauce, heat the oil in a heavy-based pan over a moderate heat. Add the onion and cook for 3 minutes, stirring constantly. Add the garlic, salt and pepper, and cook for a further 2 minutes, then add the tomatoes and bring to the boil. Reduce the heat to a simmer and cook for a good 20 minutes, stirring occasionally. Take the pan off the heat and leave to cool. (This recipe will give plenty of leftovers for another day.)

To make the dough, mix together the water, yeast and sugar, and leave to sit for 10 minutes. Place half the flour in a mixing bowl with a dough hook and pour in the liquid. Beat at medium speed for 10 minutes, then leave somewhere warm for 10 minutes.

When the mixture has become foamy, add the rest of the flour, salt and olive oil and beat for a further 5 minutes. Put the dough in a well-oiled bowl, cover with a cloth, and place somewhere warm until the dough has doubled in size (about 30 minutes).

Slap the dough down and knead for 4 minutes until soft but not too elastic. Separate into six equal pieces and roll them into balls, then leave to rest for 10 minutes.

Heat the oven to the highest temperature possible and put the trays for baking the pizzas in the oven to get very hot. With a well-floured rolling pin, flatten each ball and roll it out as thinly as possible. Take the trays from the oven, lightly oil them and dust with a little flour. Lay the dough on the hot trays. Spoon on a little of your tomato sauce, spreading it out, then scatter with the bresaola. Tear up the mozzarella and scatter it over the pizzas. Cook in the oven for about 10 minutes.

'BRESAOLA & ROAST RED PEPPER SALAD'

3 large red peppers
4 red onions
1 garlic clove
50ml olive oil, plus extra to
    serve
32-40 slices bresaola
100g watercress
50g parmesan cheese shavings
black pepper
bread, to serve

You can really cheat at this one by buying the ready-roasted peppers sold in jars all over the place. I like a bit of watercress with a good drizzle of olive oil in this salad. It doesn't need much else except a group of hungry people to devour it.

Heat the oven to 200°C (gas 6) and put the peppers, red onions, garlic and olive oil in a roasting tin. Place on the top shelf of the oven and cook for 15 minutes, then turn the vegetables and cook for a further 20 minutes. The peppers should be dark on the outside – remove them, place in a mixing bowl and cover with cling film. Return the onions to the oven for another 15 minutes.

When the onions are done, set them aside to cool a little. Remove the cling film from the peppers and cut them down the centre, discarding the seeds and core. Peel off the skin, cut the flesh into quarters and return it to the bowl with all the pepper juices. Pop the onions from their skins, cut them into quarters and mix with the peeled peppers and juice.

On a large plate, start piling up all the remaining ingredients, mixing them with the roasted vegetables. Finish with a good grind of pepper and a trickle of olive oil and serve with big hunks of crusty bread.

ALSO GOOD WITH BRESAOLA: Olive oil and shaved truffles 🐄 Rocket and buttered toast 🐄 Big wallys and mustard mayonnaise 🐄 Watercress,

'BRESAOLA WITH ASPARAGUS VINAIGRETTE'

2 bunches asparagus, or 32
   spears
salt
20 slices bresaola
1 handful chervil leaves

vinaigrette
200ml extra virgin olive oil
100ml red wine vinegar
1 tsp balsamic vinegar
1 tsp dijon mustard
salt and pepper

Asparagus spears have a tough base and a tender stem and tip. Towards the base where the white starts to turn to green, they will naturally snap. Break each one individually and set aside.

Fill a pot with cold water, add a good teaspoon of salt and bring to the boil. Tie the asparagus into bundles of 12 (or thereabouts) with kitchen twine – don't tie too tightly or it will damage the flesh. Drop the bundles into the boiling water, return to the boil and cook for 4 minutes – no longer or the flesh will be sloppy and the tips will disintegrate.

To make the vinaigrette, mix all the ingredients in a jar and shake it like mad. When the asparagus has cooked, mix it with the vinaigrette.

Lay the bresaola out on serving plates and drop the asparagus on top. Garnish with the chervil and drizzle over the remaining vinaigrette before serving.

torn mozzarella 🐄 Roast tomatoes and shaved parmesan 🐄 Hot horseradish and beetroot 🐄 Shaved pecorino and herb salad

'PASTRAMI'

salt beef, made with brisket
  (page 166)
100g salt
2 tbsp smoked paprika
100g coriander seeds
60g soft brown sugar
20g cracked black pepper
2 tbsp yellow mustard seeds
250g lapsang souchong tea

Pastrami is wonderful served simply with good bread, cornichons and piccalilli (page 184). You can buy the green wood chips for smoking the beef via the internet – you'll need a 300g bag.

First you have to make salt beef using brisket, which will take at least 4 days. Once you are ready to proceed with making pastrami, take a mortar and pestle and crush the salt, smoked paprika, coriander seeds, sugar, pepper and mustard seeds together – the mixture should just be crushed, not powdered.

Set up a smoker, or use a barbecue that has a tight-fitting lid. Make a small fire out of very good-quality wood and let it burn down to glowing coals. Mix the tea and 300g green wood chips together and place them on top of the glowing coals.

Rub the meat all over with the spice mixture and place on a flat rack in the smoker or barbecue. Cover with the lid and seal the whole thing with foil. Leave the meat to smoke for 2 hours, then open and turn it over, reseal and smoke for another 2 hours.

'PICCALILLI'

Makes 15 x 500g jars

500g table salt
2.5kg courgettes
2.5kg cauliflower
2kg frozen baby onions
500g caster sugar
125g plain flour
5 tbsp English mustard powder
4 tbsp ground turmeric
1½ tbsp ground ginger
2 litres white wine vinegar

This is the recipe we use at Smiths. It makes a lot but once in jars it lasts for ages.

Combine 4.5 litres water and the salt in a very large pot and bring to the boil, stirring until all the salt has dissolved. Leave this brine to cool.

Cut the courgettes into chunks the size of your thumbnail, and cut the cauliflower into tiny florets. Add the baby onions, courgettes and cauli to the pot, weight them down with a plate or a lid that's just smaller than the width of the pot and leave for 24 hours.

Drain the brine from the vegetables and discard it, then rinse the veg briefly under cold water and put them in a large bowl.

Put the sugar, flour, mustard, turmeric, ginger and vinegar in a pot and heat gently, stirring until thoroughly blended. Pour the spice mixture over the brined vegetables and mix very well. Spread the piccalilli out on trays and leave it to cool.

Pour the piccalilli into sterilized jars and seal. Tie some ribbon around the jars, take them to the farmers' market and sell for £12.50 (just joking).

'JOHN'S BIG TASTY PASTRAMI SANDWICH'

600g round crusty Italian bread

250g green olives stuffed with pimientos, chopped

3 large garlic cloves, chopped

1 large handful chopped flat-leaf parsley

100ml olive oil

2 tbsp white wine vinegar

200g tinned artichoke hearts, drained and halved

200g mozzarella, sliced

100g pitted black or kalamata olives, chopped

200g pastrami, sliced

200g provolone or jarlsberg cheese, sliced

200g roasted red peppers, chopped

This is muffaletta – basically a big sandwich filled with lots of meat and cheese. It travels very well and once at the spot of your picnic or family outing can be cut to feed the hungry hordes. Add whatever fillings you like – the Americans use lots of meat; the famous New Zealand chef Peter Gordon uses beetroot. The roasted peppers can be done at home or you can use the bottled Spanish ones in oil or brine. This is both fun to make and fun to eat.

Cut the loaf in half horizontally and scoop out a little of the bread inside to make some room for the filling. Mix the green olives with the garlic, parsley, olive oil and vinegar.

Spoon half the olive mixture into the bottom of the loaf, followed by all the artichokes, sliced mozzarella, then the black olives and some pastrami. Add the provolone or jarlsberg, followed by the rest of the green olives, then the roast peppers. Top with the last of the pastrami.

Place the top half of the loaf on top, tucking in all the filling. Use a tea towel to secure the two halves together, ensuring nothing can leak out the sides, then add a second layer of cloth.

Turn the loaf upside down and place it in the fridge with a few plates stacked on top to weigh it down and compress the bread into the filling. Leave for 2 hours and eat within a day, cutting the loaf into wedges to serve.

VEAL

I love beef in all its guises and that includes veal. Veal is a by-product of the dairy industry; male dairy animals don't produce milk and don't grow into great beef, but they do make great veal. In Australia (and Italy, and France) there is no stigma attached to veal as there has been in the UK. That's because until recently well-reared British veal has not been available. Now, however, thanks to public pressure, British farmers have begun producing beautiful veal out in the open. Some is light pink (it's from the younger vealers) while some is slightly darker and now marketed as rose veal (I'd call it yearling beef, but that's ok, it works for all the recipes). Crating veal animals is not allowed in the UK, but to ensure you are buying well-reared British veal you will need to find a good butcher and ask them where their veal comes from.

'HOW TO COOK VEAL CHOPS'

Grilled veal chops are wonderful – soft, sweet and delicious, and not at all just a boy's meal. Cooking them is not difficult – you just need to trust yourself and be confident. You can pan-fry or griddle them, and the following rules apply to both methods. Remember that a veal chop is a chop, a chop has a bone in it, and that bone is big. Given plenty of time and constant heat the bone will conduct heat right down to the t-junction but it needs a constant, not-too-hot heat.

Heat your pan to bloody hot and turn the oven on to 190°C (gas 5). As with a good steak, oil the meat, not the pan, then season it. Lay the chop on the pan and let it sizzle, really sizzle, for 2 minutes and then turn. (If the meat is stuck to the pan it is not ready to turn, which means the pan was not hot enough, you donkey.)

Once you've turned it cook for another 2 minutes. Turn again and pop the lot in the oven to roast for 8 minutes. Take it out of the oven, turn once more and leave the veal to rest in the pan off the heat for 3 minutes.

The juice that will be left in the pan is delicious, so after resting you can take the chop out, place the pan back on the heat and add a good lump of butter the size of your thumb. Let it melt with the pan juices and, when it has all melted and starts to bubble, squeeze in the juice of half a lemon, then serve.

'JOHN'S SOFT POLENTA'

300ml milk
½ tsp salt
¼ tsp pepper
1 garlic clove, crushed
100g instant polenta
120ml double cream
20g parmesan cheese, grated
70g mascarpone

Put the milk in a large saucepan with the salt, pepper, garlic and 200ml water and bring to a rolling boil. Sprinkle in the polenta, stirring all the time with a wooden spoon, and keep stirring until the mixture returns to the boil. Cook for 45 minutes over a very low heat, stirring often and in one direction only, otherwise you will let the evil spirits escape.

Add the cream and parmesan and cook until the cheese dissolves. Remove the pan from the heat and mix in the mascarpone.

To serve with veal, warm some serving plates. Take a big spoonful of the soft, hot polenta and drop one onto each plate. Sit your veal chops on the polenta and pour over any pan juices. Serve with half a lemon each. Simple.

'GINGER SPICED CHICKPEAS'

200g dried chickpeas, or 500g
   canned chickpeas
100ml vegetable oil
60g fresh ginger, peeled and
   pounded to a paste
1 tbsp cayenne pepper (optional)
1 tbsp ground cumin
1 tbsp ground coriander
2 tsp salt
1 x 400g can chopped tomatoes
salt and pepper
1 handful coriander leaves,
   chopped

I first ate a dish similar to this in a little café in Sydney. The only cooking medium they had was two burners on a stove and a microwave, but the food was always fabulous. The chickpeas were originally served with chicken but I have grown to love them in other ways.

Chickpeas are a great alternative to starchy foods like potato or pasta, and this dish can be made a day, or even a few days, in advance and kept in the fridge where the flavour will improve. Just remember to reheat them gently so as not to boil the flavour away. The kick from the cayenne pepper is optional but I think it adds to the overall dish, so please give it a go. You can reduce or increase the quantity, depending on how hot you like your food.

If you are using dried chickpeas, soak them in water overnight, then drain and bring to the boil in plenty of fresh water – without salt – and cook for about 2 hours, or until tender. Remove the pan from the heat and drain the chickpeas, reserving 300ml of the cooking liquid. If using canned chickpeas, drain them, reserving the liquid from the can and make it up to 300ml with water.

Place a heavy, deep frying pan or sauté pan over a medium heat and add the oil. Let it heat for 2 minutes, then throw in the ginger, spices and salt and cook for 2-3 minutes, stirring continuously, until coloured. Add the chickpeas, tomatoes and the reserved cooking liquid. Increase the heat, bring the pan to the boil and cook for 10 minutes.

Remove the pan from the heat. Add the chopped coriander and stir well. Taste and adjust the seasoning as necessary and serve alongside your veal chops. If you make the chickpeas in advance and let them cool, remember to reheat gently before serving.

'BROAD BEAN MASH & PECORINO'

300g podded broad beans,
about 2kg whole beans, frozen
if liked
50g mascarpone
50g pecorino cheese, grated
salt and pepper

This is a terrific accompaniment to veal, the flavour is full and the consistency creamy. It is also great served with a piece of fresh fish and a hunk of lemon.

Bring a large pot of water to the boil. Add the broad beans and cook for 5 minutes, then drain and cool under cold running water.

Take each broad bean and squeeze one end so that the inner bean pops out from the tough skin. Continue, discarding the skins, until all the beans are peeled (fun with the kids).

Heat the mascarpone in a small, heavy saucepan. Add the pecorino, then the beans and stir well. Season to taste. Place the creamy cheesy beans in a blender and whiz to a rough paste.

ALSO GOOD WITH VEAL CHOPS: Mashed potato and ceps bordelaise sauce and straw potatoes 🐄 Just mustard and chips 🐄 Grilled mushrooms,

'GRILLED VEAL CHOPS WITH PEAS, ARTICHOKES & BACON'

100ml extra virgin olive oil
1 large shallot, diced
1 garlic clove, minced
4 rashers streaky bacon, diced
200g peas (oh, use frozen)
4 artichoke hearts in oil,
  chopped
salt and pepper
4 veal loin chops
a little fresh thyme, leaves
  picked
50g butter

Heat the olive oil slowly in a saucepan or frying pan. Add the shallot and garlic and cook very gently for 10 minutes, stirring occasionally, then add the bacon and cook for 5 minutes more. Drain off the oil and keep it for cooking the chops. Stir the peas into the pan, then the artichokes. Season to taste with salt and pepper and keep at room temperature.

Heat a griddle pan until it is very hot. Rub the veal chops with the flavoured oil and season well with salt and pepper. Turn the oven on to 200°C (gas 6).

Griddle the chops for 2-3 minutes on each side and give them plenty of colour – they work well when a little charred. Then transfer them to the oven to continue cooking – about 3-4 minutes for medium-rare. Leave the chops to rest before serving with the peas, artichokes and bacon.

🐄 Fried potatoes with capers and lemon 🐄 Béarnaise sauce chopped parsley and olive oil 🐄 Fried egg and tomato sauce

'ROAST RUMP WITH SAUCE SOUBISE'

1 top rump (quasi) of veal,
    about 1.5kg
100ml olive oil
salt and pepper
1 leek
3 carrots
1 small bunch rosemary
375ml white wine

sauce soubise

4 small onions
1 bay leaf
1 tsp vinegar
20g butter
20g plain flour
200ml milk
100ml cream
salt and white pepper

A real blast from the past, this recipe has a great basic pot-roasting method that can be used for most meats, but especially those cuts that would dry out if simply roasted. The sauce is a classic white onion sauce, French you may gather. Use small onions rather than large ones as the bigger they are, the sweeter they get, and you don't want vanilla ice cream with your veal.

Heat the oven to 200°C (gas 6). Rub the veal with the oil, then season with lots of salt and pepper. Cut up the leek and carrots and put them in the bottom of a large lidded casserole. Sit the veal on top. Add the rosemary, then the wine and a little water. Cover and put the casserole over a high heat. Once it's boiling, transfer it to the oven and cook for 50 minutes.

Raise the heat to 220°C (gas 7), take off the lid, and continue cooking the veal for a further 20 minutes.

Meanwhile, make the sauce. Peel and slice the onions and put them in a large, heavy saucepan with the bay leaf, vinegar, butter and 200ml water. Bring to the boil over a high heat – the idea is to cook the onions, boiling off the water so they are left in some butter. Once the water has all evaporated, the butter will start to sizzle, but we don't want any colour on the onions.

Stir in the flour, then the milk. Bring to the boil and stir and stir, then take the pan off the heat. Transfer the sauce to a food processor and blend until smooth. Return it to a clean saucepan and bring to a simmer. Add the cream, then taste and adjust the seasoning as needed. Serve with the veal and lots of green peas.

'VEAL ESCALOPE WITH LEMON'

4 veal fillets, about 125g each
4 tbsp vegetable oil
60g plain flour
salt and pepper
60g butter
3 lemons, halved

Dipped in seasoned flour before frying, the meat in this recipe is substantial enough to be served alone with just a little simple salad or some sliced fresh tomatoes and basil. V good. You can use the same method for pork fillet.

To make the escalopes, sandwich each piece of fillet between two pieces of cling film and, using a rolling pin, gently flatten the meat so it is about 5mm thick. Set aside.

Heat a large frying pan over a high heat and add the vegetable oil. Season the flour with salt and pepper and turn the veal in it until evenly coated. Place the escalopes in the pan and cook over a high heat for 1 minute. Reduce the heat to medium and cook for a further 2 minutes until golden on the underside. Turn and cook for a minute or so on the other side.

Take the escalopes from the pan and set aside. Leave the pan on the heat, add the butter and season with some pepper. Let the butter melt and, as it starts to sizzle, squeeze in the juice of two of the lemon halves.

Put the escalopes onto hot serving plates, add the sauce from the pan and serve with a lemon half on each plate.

'BASIC RECIPE: CRUMBED VEAL ESCALOPES'

100g plain flour
salt and pepper
2 eggs
a little milk
200g fine, dry breadcrumbs
4 flattened veal escalopes, about
   the size of your hand
vegetable oil, for frying

What is important is that these little morsels are cooked fairly quickly, so that the meat cooks in the centre to pink but the breadcrumbs stay beautifully golden and crisp. (Yes they have to be crisp – no soggy escalopes thanks.)

Put the flour a bowl and season it well with the salt and pepper. Beat the eggs and milk together in another bowl. Set these in a line with the flour first and the breadcrumbs last in a third bowl.

Working one escalope at a time, roll the veal in the flour, then dip it into the egg. Lift, let the excess egg drain off the meat, then roll the veal in the breadcrumbs. Pat each one down firmly, making sure it is thoroughly coated with crumbs. (You may find it easier to do them all in flour, then all in egg, and then all in crumbs.)

Heat the oven to 150°C (gas 2). Put a large, heavy frying pan on the stove and get it hot. Add 2 tablespoons of oil and, once the oil is hot, drop in two escalopes (if they fit of course – I am hoping that your pan is big enough to get a couple of these things in it). They should sizzle a little. Cook for a good 4 minutes each side until they are golden – not dark brown, so either lower or increase the heat to get the desired effect.

Put the cooked escalopes in the oven to keep warm and repeat the process with the remaining escalopes, adding more oil only if necessary. Serve with the broad bean and pecorino mash (page 194), or one of the ideas on the following pages.

Tomato Sauce & Gruyère Cheese

The secret here is to buy good quality Italian tomatoes as some brands contain a lot of water.

60ml olive oil
1 onion, diced
1 garlic clove, crushed
1 tsp sea salt
1 tsp ground black pepper
700g canned chopped tomatoes
8 slices gruyère cheese

In a heavy saucepan, heat the oil over a moderate heat. Add the onion and cook for 3 minutes, stirring constantly. Add the garlic, salt and pepper and cook for a further 2 minutes. Stir in the tomatoes, bring to the boil, then simmer for a good 20 minutes, stirring occasionally.

Heat the grill. Pop a big spoonful of the sauce on top of the crumbed veal, then cover with gruyère. Put them all under the grill and cook them the way you like – either until just melted, or until really melted and bubbling and crisp. Serves 4 with some sauce leftover for something else.

Rocket, Parmesan & Capers

Fresh, salty and quick, this is a great way to eat breaded veal. The salad has a kick from the peppery rocket and sharp, vinegary capers.

200g rocket
about 100g parmesan cheese, grated or shaved
25g capers in brine
50ml olive oil
lemon wedges

Mix the rocket, cheese, capers and oil together in a bowl, adding a teaspoon of the brine from the caper jar too. Toss well and – hey ho – you're ready to serve it with the crumbed veal and lemon. Serves 4.

Chopped Boiled Eggs with Anchovies & Parsley

100g stale bread, with crusts, finely diced
1 tsp salt
1 tbsp oil or lard
2 rashers streaky bacon, chopped
6 anchovies
1 garlic clove, crushed
1 chilli, chopped
2 hard-boiled eggs, chopped
1 large handful chopped parsley

Put the diced bread in a bowl and add the salt. Sprinkle with water, then toss the bread cubes until they are uniformly damp, but not soaked. Cover tightly and leave to stand for 1 hour.

In a frying pan, heat the oil or lard. Fry the bacon and anchovies until browned, then remove them from the pan. Add the garlic, chilli and bread to the fat and fry, turning with a spatula, until the bread cubes are loose and lightly toasted.

Stir in the chopped egg, parsley, bacon and anchovies and serve with the veal. Serves 4.

Garlic Butter

Just saying 'garlic butter' takes me back to 17 years of age and my first job, where the first thing I did each day was prepare the garlic bread with lashings of garlic butter. This recipe makes a lot as I think it's worth it: the butter will keep in the fridge for a week or so.

3 garlic cloves, smashed and peeled
salt
2 tsp Worcestershire sauce
150g salted butter
1 handful finely chopped parsley

Sprinkle the garlic with some salt and crush to a paste using the flat side of a large knife. Mix with the Worcestershire sauce.

Use an electric mixer to beat the butter until it turns white and fluffy, scraping down the sides of the bowl frequently. Add the garlic mixture and parsley and beat well.

Shape the mixture into quenelles to serve on top of your veal, and wrap the rest up like a sausage in cling film to store in the fridge for another day.

Crisp Fried Potatoes & Mayonnaise

2 tbsp olive oil
500g Jersey Royal potatoes, scrubbed and halved
2 tbsp butter
2 tsp capers
juice of ½ lemon
roughly chopped tarragon
salt and pepper
mayonnaise
lemon wedges

Heat the oil in a large cast-iron frying pan. Add the potatoes and sauté until golden, then continue cooking for approximately 10 minutes, stirring all the time. The potatoes will caramelize and taste sweet.

Add the butter and capers and fry for 1-2 minutes, until the capers start to pop and become crisp. Add the lemon juice, tarragon and salt and pepper, then serve the potatoes with the veal escalopes, plus some mayonnaise and fresh lemon wedges. Serves 4.

Lemon & Parsley Butter

Great lemon and parsley butter is not greasy, it is fresh, vibrant and light, and the acid content makes it one of the very best things to serve with crumbed veal.

200g butter, cut into small cubes
salt
1 glug white wine
1 large lemon, squeezed at room temperature to get out all the juice
1 large handful chopped parsley
lemon wedges

Heat a frying pan until really hot, then add the butter and a sprinkle of salt. Pour in the wine as the butter starts to melt – it should melt fast and sizzle, if not your pan is not hot, is it?!

Once the wine is in and the butter starts to bubble, add the lemon juice and bring the pan to the boil. Stir in the parsley, pour the sauce over the veal and serve with more lemon. Serves 4.

Hollandaise sauce

You don't have to refer to the recipe on page 132 because we've got it for you right here!

6 tbsp white wine
6 tbsp white wine vinegar
20 black peppercorns
2 bay leaves
3 egg yolks
300g warm melted butter
1 pinch salt
juice of ½ lemon

Boil the first four ingredients in a saucepan for 5-8 minutes, until reduced to 3 tablespoons. Leave to cool, then strain off the flavourings.

Put the yolks in a heatproof bowl over a pan of steaming water. Whisk in a tablespoon of the vinegar mixture. Keep whisking until the sauce turns pale and the whisk leaves a pattern in it. Take the bowl from the heat and whisk in the butter. Add a tablespoon of water if you feel the sauce is about to scramble. Beat in the salt and lemon juice and keep warm until ready to serve. Serves 4.

Fried Egg & Anchovies

This great veal dish is named Holstein after the dairy cow that is the main source of veal. I love my fried eggs with crisp edges and the way to make that happen is as follows.

some oil, preferably olive
4 eggs
8 anchovies

Heat the oil in a large non-stick frying pan until quite hot. Drop your eggs in and let them start to spit and splutter – that is all part of the plan.

Next reduce the heat to low and cook until the white sets, then right at the last minute turn the heat up to full and cook for 30 seconds.

Place one fried egg on each piece of veal and lay on a couple of anchovies. There you have it. Serves 4.

'CRUMBED VEAL WITH SPAGHETTI & TOMATO SAUCE'

200g spaghetti

salt and pepper

50ml olive oil, plus extra for boiling

250g cherry tomatoes

1 garlic clove, chopped

1 handful chopped parsley

20g parmesan cheese shavings

Spaghetti is a classic Italian accompaniment to crumbed veal. To speed up the process, use your kettle to boil the water for cooking the pasta.

Fill a pot with 2 litres of water from the kettle and place over a high heat. Cook the pasta according to the packet instructions with some salt and a little oil.

In another pan, heat the olive oil with the cherry tomatoes, using the back of a spoon to squash the tomatoes so they pop. Cook for 2 minutes, then add the garlic and season with salt and pepper.

Drain the pasta and add it to the tomato sauce. Stir it through, then throw in the parsley and stir again. Sprinkle with the parmesan shavings, finish with black pepper, and serve hot alongside your crumbed veal escalopes.

ALSO GOOD WITH ESCALOPES: Wild mushrooms, parsley and shallots 🐄 Stuffed with ham and cheese 🐄 Cream and mushroom sauce

'TOMATO, OLIVE & LEMON SALAD'

4 large plum tomatoes
100g small purple or black olives
1 large handful flat-leaf parsley
2 small shallots, thinly sliced
sea salt and pepper
1 lemon
50ml good quality extra virgin
olive oil

Cut the tomatoes into chunks the size of a Lego block. Put the olives on a board and, using the palm of your hand, push down to squash each olive then remove the stone. Take the parsley and roughly chop it on the same board, so it takes up the olive juice.

Put the tomatoes in a mixing bowl with the shallots. Give them a good grind of pepper and a sprinkle of sea salt. Finely grate the zest from the lemon and add to the bowl, then squeeze the juice and add it too. Stir well and leave for 10 minutes. Add the olives, parsley and olive oil and away you go.

'VEAL SALTIMBOCCA'

8 slices parma ham
8 small veal escalopes about the
size of the palm of your hand
pepper
8 sage leaves
40ml olive oil
100g butter
juice of 1 large lemon, plus 4
lemon wedges to serve

Translated literally as 'jump in the mouth', saltimbocca is traditionally served alone.

Lay two slices of parma ham out on a flat clean surface and place an escalope in the centre of each slice. Season the meat with pepper only as the ham is salty. Stick a sage leaf on top of each escalope, then carefully fold the ham over the veal so it starts to wrap it but not tightly. Repeat until all the veal is parceled up and place all the meat in the fridge for a good 10 minutes to set.

Heat the oven to 150°C (gas 2). Sit a heavy-based frying pan over a high heat. If it is not large enough to cook all the veal parcels at one time, work in batches. Pour a little oil into the hot pan and carefully drop in the parcels. Sear for 2 minutes on each side, then remove and keep warm in the oven while you fry the others.

Once all the parcels are keeping warm in the oven, keep the frying pan over the heat and drop in the butter. When it's half-melted, squeeze in the lemon juice. Drizzle the sauce over the veal and serve two per person with a wedge of lemon.

'VEAL ESCALOPE WITH EGG & PARMESAN'

2 eggs
4 anchovies packed in oil, finely
  chopped
175g parmesan cheese, grated
½ handful chopped flat-leaf
  parsley
pepper
60g rocket
4 tbsp olive oil
4 tbsp vegetable oil
4 veal escalopes, 125g each
60g plain flour
60g butter
2 tsp white wine vinegar
1 lemon, quartered

This is my mate – I love it and cannot eat enough of it. Dipped in a light frying batter, the veal in this recipe is substantial enough to be served alone, with just a little rocket salad for accompaniment. Serve it as a winter lunch, or a main course at supper. Pork fillets can be used in place of veal. (Noooooooooo!!)

Whisk the eggs together for 1 minute until light. Stir in the anchovies, parmesan, parsley and ½ teaspoon freshly ground black pepper.

Place the rocket in the bottom of four shallow serving dishes and dress with the olive oil and some black pepper.

To cook the veal, sit two large frying pans over a high heat and add the vegetable oil. Turn the veal in the flour until evenly coated, and then dip each escalope in the cheesy egg mixture.

Place the escalopes in the pans and cook for 1 minute. Reduce the heat to medium and cook for a further 2 minutes until golden on the underside. Turn and cook on the other side for 2-3 minutes.

Add the butter to the frying pans. When it has melted, pour in the vinegar, tilting the pan to ensure the juices combine.

Lift out the escalopes and lay them on the rocket. Drizzle the veal with the buttery pan juices and serve with a big, juicy lemon wedge. You could also serve this with extra salad, if liked.

'VITELLO TONNATO'

1 egg yolk

2 tsp white vinegar

1 tsp dijon mustard

1 small tin tuna in oil, or
  100-120g leftover tuna

100ml good quality olive oil

salt and pepper

1 lemon, cut into 6 wedges

500g hunk cold roast veal

10 chives, chopped

1 loaf bread

I love the Italians. Only they would be game enough to invent a dish using leftover roast veal and leftover tuna – but hey, you have got to hand it to them, it bloody works. Soft meat and salty tuna mayonnaise – clever bastards.

Drop the egg yolk into a bowl, add the vinegar and whisk until white. Add the mustard and tuna, then drizzle in 90ml of the oil and beat to make a mayonnaise. Taste, season, then squeeze in the juice of two lemon wedges.

Slice the meat as thinly as possible and lay it out on four serving plates, or one big platter, and sprinkle with olive oil. Sprinkle over the chives, then pour the dressing over the meat in a squiggly patern, like a child making a mess. Oh yes – it's the only way to cook, like a child having fun. Much better than being stressed by it all. Add the lemon wedges and serve with the bread.

'OSSO BUCO'

4 large slices veal shin
salt and pepper
1 handful plain flour
80ml oil
2 carrots, peeled
1 onion, peeled
2 celery sticks
2 garlic cloves
2 bay leaves
1 litre beef stock (page 22), or
   other light stock

gremolata
1 handful flat-leaf parsley
1 garlic clove
1 lemon

Osso buco is a great dish of braised shin of veal. The name translates as 'bone' and 'hole' – the Italians know that works and how to sell it.

Heat the oven to 200°C (gas 6). Season the veal pieces really well. Coat them in the flour, then grind a bit more pepper over them.

Heat a large, heavy frying pan. Drop in the oil and the meat at the same time and let the veal start to brown. After 2 minutes, or when golden, turn it over and cook on the other side for the same time. Meanwhile, put all the vegetables and garlic in a food processor and make a mince out of them (or do some serious chopping).

Take the meat out of the pan and lay it in a casserole or other ovenproof dish. Add the minced vegetables and herbs to the frying pan and cook, stirring, for 5 minutes, or until the mixture is soft and smells like vegetable soup. Throw the cooked vegetables over the meat and pour the stock over the top. Cover with the lid or a sheet of foil and place in the oven for 2 hours.

While it is cooking, make the gremolata. Using a sharp knife, chop the parsley as finely as possible, then chop the garlic. Take a fine grater and remove the zest from the lemon. Combine the parsley, garlic and lemon zest in a small bowl and season with some salt and pepper. Stir well and set aside (gremolata doesn't last long so try and use it the day it is made).

Take the osso buco from the oven. I like it soupy and served with mash or rice, or just by itself, sprinkled with the gremolata. However, if you want a thicker sauce you can pour the pan-juices into a saucepan and boil until they have reduced to a thick sauce.

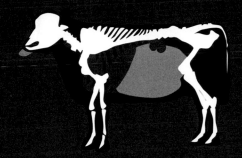

OFFAL

There are many parts of the world where offal is considered the finest of all cuts of any animal. In Thailand it is said that old recipes containing offal would have been written for the Royal palace, as all offal was reserved for the Royal family. We in the West have a varied attitude to offal – some people are scared of it and some love it. Like politics and religion, it will divide a dinner table quicker than the announcement that someone's partner is having an affair. But I do urge you to try it. Good offal is delicious (yes, really!) and so rich in flavour. Each cut requires a different cooking method but the recipes here are tasty, reliable and not over-the-top scary; I have tried to give you a gentle introduction to the subject. The sweetbreads in particular are fantabuloso.

'BASIC RECIPE: SWEETBREADS'

2-3 large sweetbreads
  (heartbreads)
1 carrot
1 celery stick
1 shallot
2 bay leaves
parsley stalks (optional)
some peppercorns
1 glug white wine
2 caps white vinegar
salt and pepper

It's funny that most people think sweetbreads are testicles – some of my family still do, no matter how many times I tell them that they don't come from anywhere near that part of the body. Sweetbreads are one of two things: they are either the gland that surrounds the heart, sometimes called heartbreads (these are about the size of your hand and really expensive), or they are thyroid glands from the throat, which are much smaller. This recipe is for the large heartbreads; if you have small sweetbreads, simply simmer them for a shorter period.

Soak the heartbreads in a bowl of cold water for 20 minutes, then drain. Use a very sharp knife to take the membrane off (this is similar to filleting a piece of fish) plus any excess fat. Put the vegetables, herbs, peppercorns, wine and vinegar in a big saucepan with 1 litre water and bring it slowly to the boil. Once it comes to the boil, sprinkle in some salt and some pepper and simmer gently for 10 minutes (or less if you are using small sweetbreads). Take the pan off the heat.

Now you have options. You can leave the heartbreads to cool completely in the cooking liquid, then slice and shallow fry them. Or, if they are to be baked whole, or wrapped in something, take them out of the cooking liquid while still hot and put them on a wire rack. Roll them in cling film so you have a tight cylinder, tie at both ends, and prick with a pin. Once they are cold, take off the cling film and cook according to the recipe you are going to use.

'FRIED SWEETBREADS, PEAS AND PANCETTA'

2 large cooked sweetbreads
(page 215)
about 50ml vegetable oil
3 shallots, diced
1 garlic clove, minced
salt and pepper
100g finely sliced pancetta, cut
into strips
300g boiled new potatoes
200g frozen peas
12 artichoke hearts packed in
oil, sliced
50g butter

Cut the prepared sweetbreads the same thickness as your thumb. Heat the oil slowly in a large frying pan and add the shallots and garlic. Cook for a few minutes, then take them out of the pan and set aside. Drop the sweetbreads into the pan, adding some more oil if needed, and leave them to cook for a good 2 minutes on each side – they must be crisp. Season the sweetbreads on both sides as they cook.

Take the sweetbreads out of the pan and set aside. Add the pancetta and potatoes to the pan and fry until coloured. Put the cooked shallots and garlic back in the pan, then add the frozen peas, artichokes and butter and warm them through. Season with some salt and pepper.

Remove the pan from the heat, add the crisp-fried sweetbreads and toss. Taste and season again if necessary, then serve.

'SWEETBREADS WITH SAUCE POIVRADE'

4 slices toasted brioche
2 large cooked sweetbreads
  (page 215)
20g butter
10ml olive oil

sauce

100g butter
400g finely diced carrots
200g finely diced celery
200g finely diced shallots
200g black peppercorns, freshly
  ground then sifted
200g redcurrant jelly
300ml malt vinegar
100ml gravy (page 33 or 153)

This pepper sauce is both sweet and hot, but also sticky. It works well cold so it doesn't matter if you have a load left over. You can also serve it with game birds and turkey, where it's far better than that bloody horrible cranberry sauce the world loves – YUK. It is important here that you sift your freshly ground peppercorns to remove the fine white innards before adding the aromatic black husks to the sauce.

Start with the sauce. Melt the butter in a saucepan. Add the vegetables and sweat until tender. Stir in the pepper and cook for another 10 minutes. Add the redcurrant jelly and malt vinegar, bring to the boil and reduce until sticky. Add the gravy, bring to the boil, then remove from the heat, taste and season.

Toast the brioche and keep it warm. Cut the sweetbreads the same thickness as your thumb. Combine the butter and olive oil in a hot frying pan. Add the sweetbreads (without seasoning them) and fry until coloured on each side.

Deglaze the pan with 75-100ml of the sauce poivrade, bring it to the boil then serve on the toasted brioche.

'SWEETBREADS IN PANCETTA WITH CHAMP & BLACK CABBAGE'

12 slices pancetta, or prosciutto
2 large cooked sweetbreads
  (page 215), wrapped in cling
  film
salt and pepper
1 tbsp olive oil
2 lemons, halved

champ

1kg potatoes, peeled
90g unsalted butter
6 spring onions
1 glug double cream

black cabbage

6 leaves cavolo nero
4 banana shallots, finely
  chopped
1 garlic clove, crushed
50g butter
splash of vegetable oil
chicken stock
1 bunch thyme, leaves picked

The idea of wrapping sweetbreads in pancetta or prosciutto is that the bacon protects the flesh and adds saltiness. I prefer pancetta because it is smokier and, because it is so thin and streaked with lard, it looks very attractive – but the choice is up to you.

Start with the champ. Put the potatoes in a large saucepan with enough cold salted water to cover. Bring to the boil and simmer for 20-25 minutes or until the potatoes are just tender.

Meanwhile, trim the cabbage leaves and wash them well. In a large saucepan, sweat the shallots and garlic in the butter and oil so that they are soft but not coloured. Add the cabbage and just enough chicken stock to cover. Bring to the boil and add the thyme. Cook uncovered for about 15 minutes, until the cabbage is tender. Season with pepper – it shouldn't need much salt. Keep warm until ready to serve.

Heat the oven to 200°C (gas 6). On a large piece of foil, lay six slices of pancetta (or prosciutto) so that they overlap each other slightly. Take the cling film off one sweetbread and season with black pepper – no salt, because the ham adds the salt. Put the sweetbread into the centre of the pancetta. Use the foil to help you roll the offal in the pancetta, making sure it is completely enclosed, and twist the ends of the foil like a sausage. Repeat with the remaining pancetta and sweetbread.

Heat the oil in a heavy-based ovenproof pan. Put the foil parcels in the pan and cook for 2 minutes or so, then turn them over and cook for about 5 minutes more.

Transfer the sweetbreads to the oven and bake for just under 10 minutes. Remove the pan from the oven and leave the sweetbreads to rest for a good 5 minutes.

Drain the potatoes well and mash them with a fork or potato masher. Mix in two-thirds of the butter and season to taste with salt and pepper. Roughly chop the spring onions, keeping the green and white parts separate.

Bring the cream and remaining butter to the boil in a medium-sized saucepan. Stir in the white parts of the spring onions and the mashed potato and stir vigorously over a medium heat for 4-5 minutes until smooth.

Remove the pan from the heat, mix in the green parts of the spring onions and season to taste. Cover and keep warm.

With a sharp knife, carve the sweetbreads into slices, cutting through the foil. Discard the foil and serve the sweetbreads with the champ, lemon halves, and a bowl of black cabbage on the side. The pancetta will be just cooked and the offal slightly pink.

Variation If you want a mashed potato recipe, follow the instructions for champ, leaving out the spring onions.

'SWEETBREAD WELLINGTONS'

300g ready-rolled butter puff
   pastry, halved
100g pâté
2 large cooked sweetbreads
   (page 215)
1 egg, beaten
mustard sauce (page 131)

Sweetbread Wellingtons are a real luxury. Many of you will know I love anything in pastry and this is no exception.

Lay the pastry pieces on the worktop and spread the pâté over them. Drop the cooled sweetbreads on top and brush all round the edges with beaten egg. Wrap the sweetbreads in the pastry, then turn them over so the seams are on the bottom. Prick the pastry parcels on top twice to let out the steam, then brush them all over with lots of egg wash. Put them on a baking tray in the freezer for 10 minutes.

Heat the oven to 200°C (gas 6) and bake the Wellingtons for 40 minutes. That's it. Slice and serve them with the mustard and cream sauce.

'OX TONGUE'

1 ox tongue
½ celeriac, peeled and chopped
1 onion, peeled and halved
2 thyme sprigs
2 bay leaves
6 peppercorns
pinch of salt

Soak the tongue in a bowl of cold water for 30 minutes to remove all the blood. Drain off the water and place in a pot. Add enough fresh water to just cover, bring to the boil, then drain and refresh under cold water. Drain well.

Put the tongue in a large saucepan, cover again with water and add the vegetables, herbs, peppercorns and a pinch of salt. Take a circle of greaseproof paper, cut a hole in the centre, and press it down onto the surface of the liquid. Bring to the boil and simmer gently for 1 hour 40 minutes. Leave the tongue to cool in the liquid.

Once the tongue is cool, peel the tongue by sliding a knife under the membrane; if properly cooked it will pull off easily.

'FRENCH DRESSED TONGUE'

200g cooked ox tongue,
    sliced (above)
4 handfuls mâche (lamb's lettuce)

french dressing
1 tsp dijon mustard
1 tbsp champagne vinegar
2 tbsp olive oil
3 tbsp vegetable oil
2 tsp hot water
salt and pepper

Put the dijon mustard in a small mixing bowl. Whisk in the vinegar slowly, followed by both oils, still whisking slowly to emulsify the dressing. Thin with the hot water and season to taste.

Finely slice the ox tongue and arrange it on four serving plates. Spoon over some of the french dressing and top each plate with a handful of mâche.

'SAUCE GRIBICHE'

4 whole hard-boiled eggs
2 hard-boiled egg yolks
½ tbsp dijon mustard
salt and pepper
½ tbsp white wine vinegar
250ml olive oil
1 bunch chervil, chopped
½ bunch tarragon, chopped
50ml capers, drained and
  chopped
100ml cornichons, drained and
  chopped

An alternative sauce for serving with tongue, this is essentially a mayonnaise in which the egg yolks are cooked instead of raw. I like to make lots and lots of it and keep it in the fridge to eat with cold ham and stuff like that. It's also good just served as a salad dressing.

Put the whole eggs and yolks, mustard and some salt and pepper in a large bowl and mash them well together. To this paste add the vinegar and then the olive oil, drop by drop as if making mayonnaise. Keep the sauce creamy by adding small amounts of vinegar or warm water, if necessary.

Finish the sauce by adding the chopped herbs, capers and cornichons. Taste and correct the seasoning as preferred.

To serve, arrange your ox tongue on plates and throw the dressing over it like a kid doing painting.

'VEAL KIDNEY WITH SPINACH & MADEIRA'

25g butter
100g spinach leaves
250g veal kidneys
vegetable oil
salt and pepper

madeira jus
200ml madeira
100ml port
100ml beef stock (page 22)

First make the madeira jus. Put the madeira, port and stock in a saucepan and bring to the boil. Boil hard until the volume has reduced to 150ml. That's it! Keep warm until ready to serve.

Meanwhile, heat the butter in a large saucepan, add the spinach and cook, stirring, until the spinach has wilted.

Heat a griddle pan until hot. Cut the kidneys into slices the width of your finger. Rub the meat with oil and add a bit of seasoning. Cook the kidneys for 2 minutes at the most on each side.

Arrange the hot buttered spinach on serving plates. Lay the kidneys on top and spoon the sauce around. Or put some sauce on the plates, top with the kidneys, then add the spinach and some more sauce. Your call.

'BAKED KIDNEY WITH MUSHROOM SAUCE'

1 whole veal kidney with fat
salt and pepper
2 tsp paprika
1 rosemary sprig

mushroom sauce
200g mixed wild mushrooms
10ml olive oil
10g butter
1 banana shallot, diced
2 tbsp crème fraîche

A whole baked veal kidney is a wonderful thing. The kidney is encased in suet and the idea is that you slowly roast the kidney in its own fat for a good hour. If you can't find a kidney with the fat still on, just spread it with a load of butter. Serve either devilled with lots of toast, or with the mushroom sauce here.

Heat the oven to 200°C (gas 6). Rub the kidney all over with salt, pepper and paprika. Lay the rosemary on a small oven tray and sit the kidney on top. Roast for a good 50 minutes to 1 hour, basting after 20 minutes and again at 40 minutes.

Clean the mushrooms by wiping them with a damp cloth. Place a large heavy pan over a high heat. Add the oil and butter, then the shallot and cook for 3 minutes until it starts to colour. Add the mushrooms and season well with pepper and salt. Cook for 4 minutes, then turn the mushrooms over and cook for a further 2 minutes. Add the crème fraîche and take the pan from the heat. Yum – mushroom sauce. Serve it with the kidney.

'TRIPE ROMAN STYLE'

2kg bleached honeycomb tripe
2 bay leaves
salt and pepper
350ml olive oil
300g carrots, diced
250g onions, diced
150g garlic, minced
250ml white wine
350g tomatoes, deseeded and
    diced
500ml gravy (page 33 or 153)
200g parmesan cheese, grated
200g pecorino cheese, grated
100g mint leaves, chopped

While working on this book, even Claire the designer, who is not a beef eater, tried this tripe dish and didn't mind the flavour, so I think you should try it too.

Put the tripe in a pot with the bay leaves and cover generously with salted water. Simmer slowly for 3 hours or until the tripe is soft. Take the tripe from the cooking liquor and let it cool before cutting it into strips the size of your little finger. Strain the broth and keep 200ml for the sauce.

Heat the olive oil in a deep, heavy-based saucepan and sauté the carrots, onions and garlic until well browned. Add the white wine and let it bubble until it has reduced to a glaze. Add the tomatoes and cook for 5 minutes.

Add the tripe, gravy and the reserved 200ml of cooking liquid. Bring to the boil and let it boil until the liquid has reduced by two-thirds in volume. Taste and adjust the seasoning, then leave the tripe to cool overnight.

When you are about to serve, heat the tripe up and boil it fast so the sauce starts to reduce and fry. Add the cheeses and cook, stirring, until the tripe is coated in the sauce and the sauce is very sticky. Add the chopped mint and serve.

'GRILLED CALVES' LIVER WITH SHERRY, BACON & SPRING ONION MASH'

1 bunch spring onions
100ml double cream
500g mashed potato
salt and pepper
12 slices streaky bacon
olive oil
4 x 150g slices calves' liver
100ml good sherry
4 handfuls watercress (optional)

Yum. Mash and liver together are great, but this sherry sauce, which is not sweet but lovely and sharp, makes this dish very cool.

Preheat the grill. Wash the spring onions and discard the outer layer, then cut the spring onions into rounds keeping the green and white parts separate.

In a stainless steel saucepan, bring the cream to the boil with the white parts of the spring onion and cook for 1 minute. Stir in the mashed potato and adjust the seasoning, mixing thoroughly. Make sure the mash bubbles and is very hot – this is comfort food and comfort food needs to be hot!

Grill the bacon until crisp and set aside until you are ready to serve (it can be reheated at the last minute if need be).

Put a griddle pan over a high heat to get really hot. Season the liver well with salt and pepper and pour over a liberal amount of olive oil. When the griddle is hot, drop the liver on it and cook over a high heat for 3 minutes on each side. Pour in the sherry and turn off the heat – the sherry should continue to bubble and start making the delicious sauce.

Mix the green parts of the spring onions with the mashed potato and place some in the centre of each serving plate. Place the liver on top, pour over the sauce from the pan and top with the bacon. Serve with watercress, if liked.

'STUFFED OX HEART'

1 large ox heart, about 1.35kg,
  split lengthways
300g stuffing mix, prepared
  according to the packet
  instructions
salt and pepper
4 tbsp vegetable oil
2 carrots, chopped
5 sage leaves
100ml beef stock (page 22)
2 tbsp red wine
1 tsp cornflour

In Australia we had colonial goose, which was a lamb shoulder stuffed and served with the leg end up to look like a goose. We also had mock goose, which was stuffed heart, and this had a deep colour and flavour. Here is a quick recipe for making it using bought dried stuffing. It works just as well for lamb hearts, just don't cook them for quite as long.

Wash the heart, trim off any excess fat and remove the arteries (your butcher should have done this already). Soak it in cold water with 2 teaspoons salt for half an hour. Take the heart out and dry it, then rub the inside and out with oil and season well with lots of pepper and salt.

Heat the oven to 140°C (gas 1). Fill the heart with the stuffing and seal the end with a skewer. Take a heavy casserole pan, heat some oil and fry the heart to seal it and give colour. Take it out and set aside. Drop the carrots into the pot, then add the sage and stock. Return the heart to the casserole then cover and place in the oven for 6 hours.

Take the heart out of the casserole and set aside. To make a sauce from the pan juices, mix the red wine into the cornflour, add the mixture to the casserole and stir over a medium-high heat until the sauce comes to the boil and thickens. Remove the sauce immediately from the heat and serve with the heart.

Tip You could simply thicken the sauce with some gravy granules instead of using the cornflour and wine.

'FAGGOTS'

225g pork mince
225g veal kidneys
225g calves' liver
40g smoked bacon
40g pork fat
75g foie gras (optional)
50g white breadcrumbs
salt and pepper
1 knob butter
2 onions, diced
5 garlic cloves, crushed
1 egg
50g sage, chopped
50g tarragon, chopped
caul fat
1 handful diced carrots
1 handful diced leek
1 handful diced celery
500ml beef stock (page 22)

Not the cleverest of names but really very tasty indeed. I was a non-offal man until I came to the UK but I have learnt that the secret is plenty (and I mean plenty) of seasoning. Faggots need lots of black pepper and salt and some herbs if you wish.

You can either ask your butcher to mince all the meat together, or place each type in the food processor separately and blend in batches. Once it is all minced, put all the meat in a large mixing bowl and mix well, beating it for a few minutes. Add the breadcrumbs and season well with lots of salt and black pepper.

Heat a frying pan over a medium heat. Add the butter, then three-quarters of the onion and sweat for 4-5 minutes, until the onion is soft but not coloured. Add the garlic and cook for another 2-3 minutes. Set aside to cool.

Stir the chopped sage and tarragon into the onions and garlic, then mix with the minced meat and place in the fridge to chill.

Heat the oven to 220°C (gas 7). Wash the caul fat and soak it in a bowl of cold water for 10 minutes, then drain thoroughly.

Lay the caul fat out on the worktop and cut it into 12-13cm squares. Roll the mince mixture into balls the size of a tennis ball then wrap each one in a piece of caul fat. Sprinkle the remaining onion and the other diced vegetables into a large roasting tray. Place the faggots on top and season them. Pour in the stock, then cover the roasting tray with foil and seal the edges well.

Put the roasting tray in the oven, reduce the heat to 180°C (gas 4) and cook for 30 minutes. Remove the foil, increase the temperature to 220°C (gas 7) and cook for a further 15 minutes. Serve with mash and onion gravy (page 33).

'SCOTCH PIES'

faggot mixture (previous page)
butter, for greasing

pastry
225g plain flour
½ tsp salt
55g beef dripping

Now this is a bit of a John Torode's version, and many people will say Scotch pies should be made with lamb, but I say 'poo poo you you'. I like the offal inside these, but they need lots of seasoning as they must be peppery. Use the faggot mixture on the previous page for filling the pies.

Make the pastry the day before baking and leave it in the fridge overnight to rest. Sift the flour and salt into a basin. Combine 150ml water and the dripping in a saucepan and stir over a medium heat until the dripping melts. Remove the pan from the heat. Make a well in the centre of the dry ingredients and add the liquid, stirring to make a dough. Wrap the pastry in cling film and leave it to rest.

Next day, heat the oven to 190°C (gas 5) and grease four 10cm baking rings to hold the pies. Roll the pastry out thinly and cut out four large rounds to be used as the bases and four smaller rounds for the tops. Put the rings on a baking sheet and use the large rounds to line the rings. Fill with the faggot mixture. Dampen the rims of the pastry cases with water, put the pastry lids on and press to seal. Cut a little hole in the top of each pie then bake for 40 minutes.

You can eat the pies hot or cold, fill the top with gravy or be really chav-tastic and put baked beans in there.

SWEET

The great Gregg Wallace, the man with whom I do *Masterchef* on telly, swears that the best desserts in the world are British, and I tend to agree. Britain's desserts are steeped in history and suet – yes, that's beef suet, the hard fat from around the animal's kidneys. The great Christmas pudding is not a great Christmas pudding without suet, the flavour is just not right. The recipes I'm giving here are stalwarts. They are not going to win any awards for flowery presentation, but they will keep you warm. I also like the idea of giving presents that I have made myself at Christmas, and mincemeat, for making mince pies, is a nice one to do.

'CLASSIC MINCEMEAT'

Makes 10 x 300g jars

1kg sour cooking apples

750g soft dark brown sugar

100ml dark rum

500g suet

grated zest of 2 lemons

grated zest of 2 oranges

2 tbsp mixed spice

2 tsp ground cinnamon

2 tsp ground nutmeg

500g mixed dried peel

500g raisins

500g sultanas

500g currants

100ml brandy

This is the basis of the great mince pie and brilliant for quick puddings like stuffed apples. Originally meat was kept in molasses and other sugars to preserve it, now the mixture is predominately dried fruit with some suet included to help preserve it and keep it moist when baked. To make mincemeat that will keep for some time you need a sink – a kitchen sink – because there are few of us with big enough bowls.

Heat the oven to 120°C (gas ¼). Peel the apples, grate them and mix with the sugar and rum in a large cast-iron casserole. Stir in the suet. Cover, transfer to the oven and cook for 4 hours, stirring the apples every hour.

Put all the rest of the ingredients, except the brandy, in the sink. Pour over the cooked apple and stir well. Leave to cool and allow the dried fruit to soak up the juices.

When it's all cool, add the brandy and stir again. Spoon the mincemeat into sterilized jars, seal and keep in a dark cool place. These make a great Christmas present, but I know what you're thinking: who has time!

'MINCE PIES'

500g shortcrust pastry
500g mincemeat (page 237)
a little milk
2 tbsp caster sugar

Mince pies for Christmas – and before. Many of us have a favourite version of this recipe. I like lots of sugar sprinkled over the top as it makes the pies sweet and the top really crunchy. They are best cooked then cooled, as the pies will have bit of juice in the bottom.

Heat the oven to 200°C (gas 6). Roll out the pastry to about 1cm thick, cut out circles slightly larger than the indentations in your bun tins (or individual pie dishes) and use them to line the tins.

Fill each pastry case almost to the top with mincemeat but leave a little room so the filling can swell a bit during cooking. Cut lids from the remaining pastry and cover the filling, pinching the edges together to seal.

Brush the tops of the pies with milk and scatter with caster sugar. Slash two slits in the crust to allow the steam to escape.

Stand your bun tins or pie dishes on a larger baking tray (in case any juice leaks out) and bake the pies for 35 minutes. Allow to cool a little before turning them out.

'CHRISTMAS PUDDING'

Makes 4 puddings

1 large white loaf bread
250g plain flour
200g suet
1 Earl Grey teabag
200ml boiling water
grated zest of 1 lemon
grated zest of 1 orange
300g mixed dried peel
200g mixed raisins, sultanas
  and currants
2 sour cooking apples, peeled
  and grated
200g blanched almonds,
  chopped
100ml brandy
750g soft dark brown sugar
2 tbsp mixed spice
2 tsp ground cinnamon
2 tsp ground nutmeg
100ml dark rum
6 eggs
450ml dark beer
butter, for greasing

Again this is a job for the sink and I suggest you make the whole amount because it is nice to give a friend a pudding at Christmas. Add a little something to make it special to you – maybe a few more nuts or chunks of dried apricot. It makes you feel good to know that you have an individual pudding.

Trim off and discard the crusts from the loaf of bread. Place the rest in a food processor and whiz to make crumbs. Mix with the flour and suet and leave somewhere warm.

In a heatproof bowl, make some tea using the teabag and boiling water. When it's ready, discard the teabag and add the zest of the citrus fruits. Put all the dried fruit, grated apples and almonds in a clean sink, pour the tea mixture over them and leave overnight.

Next day, drain any excess liquid from the dried fruit mixture and pour over the brandy. Mix the dark sugar with the spices and rum. Beat in the eggs, then add the beer. Pour the sugar and egg mixture over the fruit, add the breadcrumb mixture and mix together using both hands and arms right up to your elbows.

Butter four 1.65 litre pudding bowls and fill them with the pudding mixture. Cover with greaseproof paper and then with foil. Put a folded tea towel in the bottom of a large pot and place the pudding basins on it. Add enough water to come three-quarters of the way up the sides of the basins and boil the puddings for 3 hours, topping up the water level as necessary.

Take the puddings out of the pot and leave them to cool, then remove the foil, leaving the greaseproof paper on. Cover the basins with fresh foil or with a pudding cloth, wrap with string and store in a cool place ready for Christmas. To reheat for serving, boil as above for 1 hour.

'BAKED APPLES & CUSTARD'

120g suet
150g light brown muscovado
    sugar
200g grated bramley apples
100g sultanas
60g raisins
100g prunes, chopped
40g walnuts, chopped
40g almonds, chopped
1 tsp ground cinnamon
½ tsp mixed spice
1 generous shot dark rum
1 generous shot brandy
10 cox's apples
150g butter
icing sugar, for sifting

vanilla custard

1 litre milk
8 egg yolks
120g vanilla sugar
40g cornflour
40g plain flour
125ml brandy

This will make just over a litre of custard. If you want to halve the recipe, do, but it is delicious cold and can be re-heated for use the next day. I just find it easier to make it in large quantities, and people seem to love it so much they always want more...

Heat the oven to 200°C (gas 6). In a mixing bowl combine the suet, sugar, grated bramleys, dried fruit, nuts, spices, rum and brandy. Stir well and set aside.

Don't peel the cox's but slice off a little of the top and the bottom (so that they sit flat in a roasting tray). Halfway down the sides of the apples, make an incision all away around the middle (so that the apples don't explode as they cook). Remove the cores.

Stuff each apple with as much of the dried fruit mixture as you can get in – there will be plenty, so be generous and let some spill out over the top. Put the stuffed apples in a large roasting tin and top each one with some of the butter, pushing it in with your finger so the butter is inside. Sift some icing sugar over the top and bake for 20 minutes.

Meanwhile, make the custard. Heat the milk in a saucepan until it just comes up to the boil, then take the pan off the heat immediately. In a large heatproof bowl beat together the egg yolks, vanilla sugar, cornflour and plain flour. Pour the hot milk slowly over the egg mixture, beating well.

Return the custard to the saucepan and place over a low heat, stirring for a few minutes until the mixture thickens. Stir in the brandy. Remove from the heat and set aside in a warm place.

Take the apples from the oven. Carefully drain off the pan juices and serve them as a sauce with the baked apples and custard.

'STEAMED MARMALADE PUDDING WITH BLOOD ORANGES'

80g butter, plus extra for
  greasing
caster sugar, for dusting
100g strong marmalade
300g dark brown sugar
1½ tbsp molasses
2 eggs
½ tsp baking powder
2 tsp ground ginger
350g self-raising flour, sifted
150g suet
4 blood oranges
vanilla custard (page 240)

Cleverly disguised as an elegant, grown-up dessert, these individual puddings topped with marmalade are sticky and sweet. They really are nursery food at its very best. The hot pudding combined with the cold bitter orange and the sweet vanilla custard is a real taste treat.

Heat the oven to 200°C (gas 6). Grease eight ramekins or small pudding moulds with a little butter and sprinkle with caster sugar. Spoon a generous quantity of marmalade into the bottom of each ramekin and set aside.

In a mixing bowl, cream together the butter, dark brown sugar and molasses. Stir in the eggs one at a time, then add the baking powder and ground ginger.

In a separate bowl rub the flour and suet together. Add to the butter and egg mixture and stir well.

Spoon the batter into the ramekins so that they are three-quarters full. Put a tea towel in the bottom of a roasting tin (if using metal dishes for the puddings, this will prevent them becoming too hot). Put the puddings on top and pour in enough hot water to come halfway up the sides of the ramekins.

Bake the puddings for 40 minutes, or until they are firm to the touch. Remove from the oven and leave for 10-15 minutes to settle. If preferred, the puddings can be baked in advance and then reheated later in a 170°C (gas 3) oven for about 8 minutes, or turned out, covered with cling film and heated in a microwave oven on HIGH for 90 seconds.

Peel and slice the blood oranges and spread them out on serving plates. Gently press around the edges of the puddings with your fingertips, bringing the sides away from the moulds, and turn out onto the blood oranges. Serve with the vanilla custard.

'GOLDEN SYRUP DUMPLINGS'

250g self-raising flour
100g suet
35g caster sugar
400g golden syrup
vanilla custard (page 240) or
    pouring cream, to serve

These sweet versions of the great dumpling are cooked in golden syrup and water. The cooking liquid is reduced and poured over the dumplings before serving with custard or cream.

Mix the flour, suet and sugar together in a large bowl and stir in 100ml warm water, or enough to make a heavy dough.

In a wide saucepan, sauté pan or wok, combine the golden syrup and 1 litre water and bring to the boil. Roll the dough into balls about the size of a golf ball.

Working in batches of 12 at a time, drop the dumplings into the boiling syrup. After about 5 minutes they will float to the top, which shows that they are cooked. At this point roll them over and leave to cook for another minute or so, then remove the dumplings from the syrup and set aside while you cook the rest.

When the dumplings are all cooked, fast-boil the cooking liquid to reduce it to about 500ml. Drop all the dumplings into this sauce and toss them so they are well coated. Serve with vanilla custard or pouring cream.

Variation To make spotted dick, leave out the jam and instead add 100g sultanas to the dough. Shape it into a log and cook the same way.

'JAM ROLY POLY'

20g baking powder
200g plain flour
100g suet
50ml warm milk
grated zest and juice of 1 lemon
2 eggs
400g chunky jam
vanilla custard (page 240) or
   pouring cream, to serve

Heat the oven to 200°C (gas 6), if using. Mix the baking powder and flour together in a bowl and rub in the suet to give a mixture the texture of breadcrumbs.

In a jug, combine the warm milk, lemon zest and juice (if the milk is really hot it will curdle so be careful). Beat in the eggs, then pour the liquid into the flour mixture and stir to form a dough.

Roll the dough out to a square about 2cm thick. Cover it with greaseproof paper, and then a sheet of foil large enough to cover it generously. Flip the whole thing over so the dough is on top and spread it with the jam. Roll it all up into a big sausage shape and twist the ends of the foil to secure them.

Steam the pudding in a water-filled roasting tray in the oven, or over a pan of gently simmering water for 2 hours. You can divide the uncooked roly poly into smaller pieces to fit in a small steamer if that's all you have – they may look a bit stumpy but they will still taste great. Serve with custard or cream.

'SUSSEX POND PUDDING'

180g butter, plus extra for
    greasing
1 unwaxed lemon
200g caster sugar
soured cream or pouring cream,
    to serve

suet dough

175g flour
65g butter
65g suet
½ tsp salt
½ tsp sugar
½ tbsp warm water

Tip You could make
a similar pudding
with an orange –
perhaps a blood
orange, so you get a
lovely red colour, or
even small individual
puddings with limes
in the centre.

Soured cream is better with Sussex Pond pudding than normal runny cream, but make your own mind up.

Mix all the ingredients for the dough together, kneading lightly until you have a smooth dough. Try not to over-work it or the heat of your hands will melt the suet and the crust will not be springy.

Roll out one-third of the dough into a circle large enough to cover the top of an 800ml pudding basin and set side. Grease the inside of the bowl with a little butter. Cut a circle of greaseproof paper to fit the bottom of the bowl. Moisten it with water to make it more pliable and press inside. Roll out the remaining piece of dough into a circle big enough to line the pudding basin, leaving a small overhang around the top. Press the dough gently into the basin.

Spike the rind of the lemon all over with a fork. Put about 90g butter inside the dough-lined basin, cover with 100g caster sugar, then wedge the lemon upright in it. Cover with the same amount of sugar and another 90g butter.

Put the pastry lid on top of the pudding and bring the overhang over the top. Moisten the underside with a little water and press gently to seal. Cover the top of the pudding with a double sheet of greaseproof paper, again moistened with water, and tie with string to keep it in place. Finally, wrap the whole thing with foil.

Put a folded tea towel inside a large pan and sit the pudding on top. Carefully add enough boiling water to come three-quarters of the way up the side of the basin. Cover and simmer for 2½ hours, topping up with extra hot water when necessary. During cooking, the sugar, lemon juice and butter will seep into the crust.

Remove the pudding from the heat and take off the foil and paper. Turn out the pudding, cut a big wedge for each person, and serve it hot with soured cream or regular cream.

'CLOOTIE PUDDING'

100ml warm milk
½ x 454g can golden syrup
1 tsp ground ginger
1 tsp ground cinnamon
2 eggs, lightly beaten
250g mixed sultanas and
  currants
2 carrots, grated
350g plain flour, plus 1 tbsp for
  the cloth
3 tsp baking powder
100g caster sugar
100g pinhead oatmeal
150g suet
vanilla custard (page 240)

This little number has many variations – some with grated apple, some with carrot, and many with a lot more spicing. However, the fact remains that it is the Scottish version of the Christmas pudding. Like Christmas Pudding, it is wrapped in cloth and boiled, but many people then cool it and cut it into slices or wedges, then pour over a shed load of custard and bake the whole lot for about 30 minutes, giving a baked custard pudding stodgy dumpling thing. Hey – the Scots have to keep warm after all.

Warm the milk in a large saucepan. Add the golden syrup and spices, then take the pan off the heat. When it's coolish, add the beaten eggs, dried fruit and grated carrots.

Sift together the flour and baking powder then add the sugar, oatmeal and suet and rub together until well combined. Add the wet ingredients to the dry and mix well together.

Lay a pudding cloth on the work bench, pile the mixture into the middle and wrap it up. Cook in a steamer over boiling water for a good 3 hours, then take the pudding out and leave it to cool.

Heat the oven to 170°C (gas 3). Cut the pudding into slices, put them in a baking dish and cover with custard. Bake for 30 minutes until the custard is bubbling and brown on top.

'SWEET YORKSHIRE PUDDINGS WITH DAMSON JAM & CLOTTED CREAM'

jam
1.8kg damsons or plums
1.8kg sugar

clotted cream
750ml double cream
25g butter
1 vanilla pod (optional)

Yorkshire puddings
8 eggs
600ml milk
500g plain flour, sifted
3 tbsp dripping
icing sugar, sifted

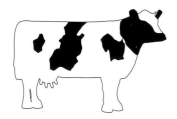

Now you can either use your leftover Yorkshires to make this lovely pud, or start the batter from scratch leaving out the salt. The jam recipe makes around 2.7kg, or you could of course use some good quality ready-made jam (raspberry is good).

To make the jam, wash and wipe the fruit and cut them in half. Put them into a large pan with 575ml water and simmer gently until the fruit is soft. Add the sugar and stir until it dissolves.

Bring the jam to the boil, removing any stones and froth as they rise to the surface, and boil rapidly until the jam reaches setting point. To test this, put a blob of jam on a chilled plate and put it in the fridge for a few minutes – setting point is reached when you push your finger into the blob and the surface wrinkles.

When the jam is ready, skim it once more, then pour into sterilized jars and seal while still hot.

To make the clotted cream, mix the double cream and butter in a heavy pan and bring to a simmer over a medium heat. Stir it constantly with a wooden spoon and, about 8 minutes later, the volume of cream should be almost half what it was when you started. If liked, add the vanilla towards the end of this process. Pour the cream into a flat dish and leave to cool in the fridge.

To make the Yorkshires, heat the oven to 220°C (gas 7). Beat the eggs with the milk, then beat the flour into the milk mixture to make a batter. Sieve it if you like. Put the Yorkshire tray in the oven until hot. Add some dripping to each indentation and heat until the fat is smoking-hot. Ladle some batter into each hole, then return the tray to the oven. Reduce the heat to 200°C (gas 6) and cook for 15 minutes.

Take the Yorkshires from the oven and put one on each serving plate. Add a big spoonful of jam to the centre, then some of the cream. Dust with plenty of icing sugar and serve hot.

'BUTCHERS'

LONDON

SC Crosby
65 Charterhouse Street,
London, EC1M 6HJ
Tel: 020 7253 1239

Dove's Butchers
71 Northcote Road,
London SW11 6PJ
Tel: 020 7223 5191

The Ginger Pig
99 Lauriston Road,
London E9 7HJ
Tel: 020 8986 6911
www.thegingerpig.co.uk

Frank Godrey
7 Highbury Park,
London N5 1QJ
Tel: 020 7226 2425
www.fgodrey.co.uk

Macken Bros
44 Turnham Gn Terrace,
London W4 1QP
Tel: 020 8994 2646

William Rose
126 Lordship Lane,
London SE22 8HD
Tel: 020 8693 9191
www.williamrosebutchers.com

THE SOUTH

Butts Farm Butcher Shop
South Cerney, Cirencester,
Gloucestershire GL7 5QE
Tel: 01285 862224
www.thebuttsfarmshop.com

Eastwoods of Berkhamsted
15 Gravel Path, Berkhampsted,
Hertfordshire HP4 2EF
Tel: 01442 865012

M Feller, Son & Daughter
54-55 Oxford Covered Market,
Oxford, Oxfordshire OX1 3DY
Tel: 01865 251164

Hayman's Butchers
6 Church Street, Sidmouth,
Devon EX10 8LY
Tel: 01395 512877

CH Wakeling
41 Farncombe Street,
Godalming, Surrey GU7 3LH
Tel: 01483 417557
www.wakelings.co.uk

Philip Warren & Son
1 Westgate Street, Launceston,
Cornwall PL15 7AB
Tel No: 01566 772089

J Wicken's Family Butchers
Castle Street, Winchelsea
Town, East Sussex TN36 4HU
Tel: 01797 226287

THE NORTH

FC Phipps
Osbourne House, Mareham-Le-
Fen, Lincolnshire PE22 7RW
Tel: 01507 568235

George Payne
27 Princes Road,
Brunton Park, Gosforth,
Newcastle-Upon-Tyne NE3 5TT
Tel: 0191 236 2992

George Scott Butchers
81 Low Petergate, York North,
Yorkshire YO1 7HY
Tel: 01904 622972

Lishman's of Ilkley
23/27 Leeds Road, Ilkley,
West Yorkshire LS29 8DP

Northumberland NE46 1NJ
Tel: 01943 609 436

Noel Chadwick
51 High Street, Standish,
Wigan WN6 0HA
Tel: 01257 421137
www.noelchadwick.co.uk

G Callaghan & Son
8 Central Square, Maghull,
Liverpool, Merseyside L31 0AE
Tel: 0151 526 9345

SCOTLAND

Macbeth's
11 Tolbooth Street, Forres,
Moray IV36 1PH
Tel: 01309 672254
www.macbeths.com

Crombie's of Edinburgh
97 Broughton Street,
Edinburgh EH1 3RZ
Tel: 0131 556 7643

D&A Kennedy
10-12 Castle Street,
Forfar, Angus DD8 3AD
Tel: 01307 462118

**Thomas Johnston Quality
Butchers**
6/8 Cow Wynd,
Falkirk FK1 1PL
Tel: 01324 623456

WALES

Edwards of Conwy
18 High Street, Conwy,
North Wales LL32 8DE
Tel: 01492 592443
www.edwardsofconwy.co.uk

HJ Edwards & Son
1-3 Flannel Street,
Abergavenny, Gwent NP7 5EG
Tel: 01873 853110

Eynon's of St Clears
Deganwy Pentre Road,
St Clears, Carmarthenshire
SA33 4LR
Tel: 0800 731 5816
www.eynons.co.uk

Edward Hamer Ltd
Plynlimon House, Llanidloes,
Powys SY18 6EF
Tel: 01686 412209
www.edwardhamer.co.uk

NORTHERN IRELAND

O'Kane Meats
Main Street, Claudy
BT47 4HR
Tel: 028 7133 8944
www.okanemeats.com

O'Doherty's Fine Meats
3 Belmore Street, Enniskillen
County Fermanagh
BT74 6AA
Tel: 028 6632 2152

FURTHER INFORMATION
UK
Rare Breeds Survival Trust
www.rbst.org.uk

The Guild of Q Butchers
www.guildofqbutchers.com

AUSTRALIA
**Rare Breeds Trust of
Australia**
www.rbta.org

**Highly Recommended
Butchers**
www.eatanddrink.com.au/food
_outlet_search.cfm

'INDEX'

Editorial Director Anne Furniss
Creative Director Helen Lewis
Project Editor Jenni Muir
Designer Claire Peters
Design Consultant Mark Harper
Photographer Jason Lowe
Props Styling Cynthia Inions
Food Stylists John Torode and
 Tony Moyse
Production Director Vincent Smith
Production Controller Ruth Deary

First published in 2008 by
Quadrille Publishing Limited
Alhambra House
27-31 Charing Cross Road
London WC2H 0LS
www.quadrille.co.uk

Reprinted in 2008
10 9 8 7 6 5 4 3 2

Text © 2008 John Torode
Photography © 2008 Jason Lowe
Design and layout © 2008 Quadrille
Publishing Ltd

Cataloguing in Publication Data: a
catalogue record for this book is available
from the British Library.

ISBN 978 184400 623 6 (UK trade edition)
ISBN 978 184400 690 8 (Export edition)

Printed in Spain

'ACKNOWLEDGEMENTS'

There would be no book without the cook, and to make that cook there has been many a patient mentor – to you all, and you know who you are, thank you. To Mark Harper, a man who laughs at my ridiculous ideas but then makes my dreams a reality – YOU ROCK, that poster boy is the best. For Claire Peters, who whilst designing this great book was converted to eating beef. For all your time and what is a beautiful book, thanks. To Jenni Muir, the straight-faced editor with a big heart and great mind: patience is a virtue and by God you're virtuous, and sometimes funny! This is a great book because of your pestering and care, thank you. Without the persistence of Anne Furniss, Alison Cathie, Helen Lewis and the team at Quadrille, this book would not be, either. Thanks for believing that a single subject book is a good thing. For all my team at Smiths of Smithfield: you are the best of the best and Smiths is all down to you. Special thanks to one man in particular, Tony Moyse – without you this book would not be, and without you Smiths would not

be what it is. You are a fab man, and thanks for letting him out, Claire. To Jessie, my missus, who made the rambling words of a mad chef into language the world would understand, and for keeping me in it – thanks Beautiful. There is also this guy who takes great photos – his name is Jason Lowe and he is really, really good. I love working with you, Jason, but next time I will insist on the watercress. The throne works as you said it would! Big ones. For all the team at *Masterchef*, in particular Gregg Wallace and his big bald head and the lovely, trusting, believing Karen Ross. Thanks for making me famous. Sometimes I like it. In this great restaurant industry, we all learn by copying each other, so thanks to all the people I have worked with and who have inspired me. Lastly, to every farmer, butcher, producer and grower – without your knowledge and love of what you do, and the lessons you have taught me, without you there would be no **BEEF**!